Latin American Monographs

Second Series

# Alejandro O. Deústua

24

Center for Latin American Studies
University of Florida

# Alejandro O. Deústua

## Philosophy in Defense of Man

## Jack Himelblau

A University of Florida Book
University Presses of Florida
Gainesville—1979

A University of Florida Book sponsored by the
Center for Latin American Studies

The University Presses of Florida is the scholarly publishing agency
for the State University System of Florida

The substance of the material in two of the chapters in this volume has appeared previously in another publication: chapter 2, in "Alejandro O. Deústua: An Aesthetic Vision of Education," *Inter-American Review of Bibliography*, 20, no. 4 (1970), 417–26, and chapter 3, in "A. O. Deústua on the Dilemma of Order vs. Liberty in Occidental Thought," *Inter-American Review of Bibliography*, 26, no. 1 (1976), 60–78.

Library of Congress Cataloging in Publication Data

Himelblau, Jack.
    Alejandro O. Deústua: philosophy in defense of man.

    (Latin American monographs; 2d ser., 24)
    "A University of Florida book."    Bibliography: p. 115
    1. Deústua, Alejandro Octavio, 1849–1945.   I.   Series:
Florida.   University, Gainesville.   Center for Latin
American Studies.   Latin American monographs; 2d ser.,
24.
B1074.D484H55        199'.85        78-25650
ISBN 0-8130-0628-7

Typography by Creative Composition Company
Albuquerque, New Mexico

Printed by Storter Printing Company
Gainesville, Florida

81-115

# Preface

Bibliography on Latin American philosophers reveals that since 1940 serious efforts have been undertaken to study in depth the intellectual currents in Argentina, Brazil, Cuba, Mexico, and Uruguay. For the most part, the philosophers who have kindled the interest of the critics have come from the two poles of the Spanish-speaking countries: from Argentina, José Ingenieros, Alejandro Korn, Alberto Rougès, and Francisco Romero; from Mexico, Antonio Caso and José Vasconcelos. With respect to Peruvian thinkers, there has been an almost total silence. Outside of Augusto Salazar Bondy's historical surveys of Peruvian philosophy, little has been written on any specific man. In fact, Salazar Bondy has commented sadly on the absence of any monograph dealing with the most notable figures of Peru's intellectual history. This is especially true in Alejandro O. Deústua's case. In Deústua one finds that rare combination of thinker and man of action at all times. He is unquestionably Peru's most distinguished philosopher and one of Latin America's foremost intellectuals and pedagogues of the first quarter of the twentieth century. The present work, then, constitutes an effort to narrow the critical gap that exists in the study of the history of ideas in Peru. There is no better way to begin such a task than to pay tribute to Deústua, who throughout his life exalted what was original, creative, and good in his fellowman.

To Anabel
for your love and support

# Contents

# Chronology

1849    Born on March 22 in Huancayo, Department of Junín, to Remigio Deústua and Toribia Escarza.

1853    Family moves to Lima.

1863    Attends the Colegio Nacional de Guadalupe.

1868    Admitted to the University of San Marcos.

1869    Receives his B.A. and is named lecturer in philosophy.

1870    Appointed interim professor of calculus and geometry at the Naval Academy Dos de Mayo in Callao by the federal government.

1871    Receives his M.A.; placed in charge of the curriculum for junior high school at Dos de Mayo.

1872    Obtains his Ph.D. in humanities and his J.D. Made first lieutenant of the Ninth Battalion of the Lima National Guard.

1873    Receives his LL.M. and LL.D. Replaces his father as marine clerk and court clerk in Callao. Named professor of philosophy and classical history by the Honorable Departmental Council of Callao in Dos de Mayo. Appointed chief of primary and secondary education in Callao. Appointed alternate senator for Callao.

1875    Becomes a member of the bar of Lima. Named editor of the important daily newspaper *El Callao* and later assumes the editorship of the dailies *El Constitucional* and *La Época*. Also collaborates as a journalist in *La Opinión Nacional* and the *South Pacific Times*.

1877 Obtains the chair of geography and history in Dos de Mayo and offers tutorials in philosophy to advanced students.

1879 His teaching and journalistic career is interrupted by the outbreak of the War of the Pacific against Chile.

1880 Participates in the disastrous Battle of Miraflores. Named chief of the Department of Statistics in addition to his prior duties as chief of primary and secondary education. Made first sergeant of the Fourth Company of the Tenth Battalion. Later promoted to first lieutenant.

1881 Named sergeant major of the infantry of the Second Battalion of the National Guard of Callao.

1882 Named adjunct professor of general literature and aesthetics in the School of Liberal Arts and Sciences at the University of San Marcos. Partakes in political campaigns, becomes a member of the Civilist party's Executive Committee, and assumes the editorship of *La Opinión Nacional*.

1884 Named full professor of aesthetics.

1888 Named full professor of literature at the Maritime School by the federal government.

1889 Named legal adviser *ad honorem* to the Maritime Superior Junta.

1891 Elected joint judge of the province of Callao.

1893 Receives the rank of lieutenant colonel and is placed second in command of the University Battalion of the National Guard of Lima.

1894 Publishes "Un juicio crítico notable," a review in the daily *El Callao* of Javier Prado y Ugarteche's book *Estado social del Perú durante la dominación española*.

1895 Begins his lifetime career as a public servant by accepting the general directorship of the Department of Justice, Culture, Education, and Welfare. Subsequently resigns from this position due to a ministerial crisis. Appointed secretary of the Peruvian delegation in the Republic of Argentina and later named to the delegation in Brazil.

1897　Named chargé d'affaires in Argentina by his government.

1898　Publishes a lengthy report entitled "La instrucción primaria en la República Argentina" in article form (1898–99). Commissioned to study the primary and secondary school systems in Europe by President Piérola.

1900　Appointed to the Peruvian delegation to the Ibero-American Congress in Madrid. Publishes "La instrucción pública en Francia" as a series of articles from 1900 to 1903 and 1907. Decorated by Queen Cristina with the medal of the Order of Knight Commander of the Catholic Queen Isabel. Elected honorary member of the Spanish Association of Writers and Artists.

1901　Elected senator to Congress from Lima. Appointed to the Superior Council of Education as the representative of the School of Liberal Arts and Sciences. Draws up a project for the reform of secondary education.

1902　Named full professor of philosophy. Resolves governmental crisis between President López de Romaña and the House of Representatives. Organizes a new cabinet and assumes the post of secretary of the interior and internal security until the close of the congressional session that year.

1905　Publishes *El problema de la educación nacional*— reprinted in 1937 as "El problema pedagógico nacional" in *La cultura nacional*.

1907　Publishes "Reforma de exámenes de la Facultad de Letras" and "Un libro notable," a review of Francisco García Calderón's book *Le Pérou contemporain*.

1908　Publishes *Apuntes sobre la enseñanza secundaria*.

Appointed confident agent to the Holy See to defend Peruvian ecclesiastical jurisdiction in Tacna y Arica.

1909   Commissioned by the minister of public education to continue his research on the public education systems in Europe.

1912   Publishes *La cultura superior en Italia*. Serves on the National Electoral Committee.

1913   Publishes "La cultura general y técnica," "Libertad y obediencia," "La escuela de cultura general," "El dualismo en el problema pedagógico," "El deber pedagógico del estado," and "Moralidad y educación."

1914   The above articles reappear in an amplified monograph entitled *A propósito de un cuestionario sobre la ley de instrucción*. (The latter is subsequently republished as "La ley de instrucción" in *La cultura nacional*.)

1915   Appointed dean of the School of Liberal Arts and Sciences at the University of San Marcos. Named delegate to the Second Pan-American Scientific Congress, held in Washington, D.C.

1916   Publishes "La reforma de la segunda enseñanza."

1917   Succeeds Ricardo Palma as director of the Biblioteca Nacional. Publishes seventeen chapters of *Las ideas de orden y de libertad en la historia del pensamiento humano* in article form from 1917 to 1922.

1919   Publishes volume 1 of *Las ideas de orden y de libertad* (chapters 1–9).

1920   Publishes "Clasificaciones estéticas," "El valor estético," "Grados estéticos," "La actividad estética," "La experiencia estética," and "Lo bello en la naturaleza."

1921   Publishes "La estética de la libertad" and "Lo bello en el arte."

1922   Publishes volume 2 of *Las ideas de orden y de libertad* (chapters 10–19).

1923   Publishes *Estética general*, "Apuntes sobre la teoría del valor," and "La belleza y el bien."

1924   Presents a paper, "La estética contemporánea," at

the Fourth International Congress of Philosophy in Naples. Publishes "Sobre la teoría del valor."

1927 Publishes *El problema universitario; la cultura universitaria en Suiza.*

1928 Becomes president of the University of San Marcos, serving until the end of the academic year 1930.

1929 Publishes *La cultura superior en Suiza* and *Estética aplicada. Lo bello en la naturaleza (apuntes).*

1930 Named adviser to the Peruvian delegation in Spain. Publishes "Informe presentado al supremo gobierno relativo a la reforma universitaria."

1932 Publishes *Estética aplicada. Lo bello en el arte: la arquitectura (apuntes y extractos).*

1935 Publishes *Estética aplicada. Lo bello en el arte: escultura, pintura y música (apuntes y extractos).*

1937 Publishes *La cultura nacional.*

1938 Publishes volume 1 of *Los sistemas de moral.*

1939 Publishes *La estética de José Vasconcelos.* Receives the Premio Roma from the Royal Academy of Italy.

1940 Publishes volume 2 of *Los sistemas de moral* and the articles "Ideas sobre la educación moral" and "La escuela de hoy y la escuela de mañana."

1945 Deústua dies August 6.

# 1. The Man and His Times

Alejandro O. Deústua stands as a living example of a life dedicated to the cause of liberty. He was, in the true sense of the word, a Renaissance man. A man of action and reflection, Deústua imposed his will on his circumstance, determining his Self in spite of it. Much like Domingo Faustino Sarmiento, the great nineteenth-century Argentinian liberal who altered the course of his country's history, Deústua was the instrument of radical transformation in Peru. Though similar in this respect, the two men differed widely with regard to the scope and purpose of their actions. Whereas Sarmiento, as a politician, directed his energies toward practical social reform, Deústua, as a philosopher, made his most valuable contributions in the arena of speculative thought.

Indeed, Deústua has been the prime mover of Peru's intellectual rejuvenation in the twentieth century. Before Deústua appeared on the national scene, Peru had muddled through a series of philosophical movements, trying to keep in step with the changing ideas of Europe. Little consideration was given to the particular American realities of Peru. Even more important, no attempt was made to impart a universal sense of self-dignity to the Peruvian in order to lift him beyond his geographical setting and to incorporate him into the mainstream of mankind as an active individual participant, as a being defined by a unique—not national—personality. The professors of philosophy at the University of San Marcos had kept alive scholasticism in deference to its Spanish past—a tradition that is still poignantly felt in the twentieth century. They lectured on the ideas of the age of reason, the age of enlightment, and the age of ideology in the sixteenth, seventeenth, eighteenth, and nineteenth centuries, respectively, as so many abstract word games. When positivism swept Peru in the late 1870s, the above picture drastically changed. The enthusiasts of this new movement, exalting materialism and scientific determinism as the road to unlimited human progress, coerced the nation into adopting foreign life styles with disastrous moral and economic effects. (Mexico and Brazil had virtually been converted to Comtian states, and Peru lagged not far behind.) Among his colleagues, Deústua was the first to perceive the ill effects that positive polity had had on his country—but only after he himself had passed through a modified yet ardent positive stage. Declaiming against positivism and the strong materialistic and antispeculative contemporary trend, Deústua proposed to replace it with a new vision of life wherein man and self-esteem—not economic wealth—occupied the center of the social stage.[1]

As a professor, Deústua's dynamic personality quickly attracted a constellation of disciples—for example, Victor D. Belaúnde, Francisco García Calderón, Mariano Ibérico, Julio Chiriboga, José de la Riva Agüero, Enrique Barboza, Oscar Miró Quesada—who were later to become the leading intellectual figures of Peru. His gifts as a teacher were readily acknowledged. Enrique Barboza, for instance, wrote of Deústua's "brilliant and unforgettable lectures."[2] Julio Chiriboga's portrait of the maestro, in turn, leaves no doubt that here was an eminent educator who, through his altruism,

1. For a historical survey of philosophic thought in Peru, see Augusto Salazar Bondy's monograph *La filosofía en el Perú: Panorama histórico* (Washington, D.C., n.d.) and his *Historia de las ideas en el Perú contemporáneo,* 2 vols. (Lima, 1965).

2. "Las ideas pedagógicas de Alejandro O. Deústua," *Letras,* 13 (1939), 162. (Translations from this journal are mine.)

optimism, and intellectual fervor as well as his devotion to and
faith in his country's youth, not only inspired a whole generation of men but also reinvigorated philosophic thought in Peru:[3]

> Su vocación de educador era tan fuerte, tan completa su
> entrega a la tarea educativa y tan hondo su amor a la
> juventud que, corridos ya muchos años, sus discípulos no
> podemos evocar la noble figura del maestro sin represen-
> tárnosla como nimbada por una especie de mística au-
> reola. Cano ya, el busto erguido, vibrante la palabra, el
> ceño adusto y la mirada encendida era como un profeta
> bíblico que, al derramar a manos llenas, los tesoros de su
> espíritu privilegiado, no veía ante sí a estos o aquellos es-
> tudiantes sino a la juventud, a la eterna juventud de la
> patria, de cuyos destinos se sentía responsable. Quería
> verla emerger del crisol de sus enseñanzas, iluminada por
> los más altos valores humanos. Patriota y visionario, la
> veía ya en la perspectiva de sus sueños, instruída, buena,
> bella y útil. ¡Y sus sueños duran todavía, alimentando la
> vida casi centenaria del maestro de maestros!

The founder of Peru's vital new philosophy was born in
Huancayo, Department of Junín, on March 22, 1849. After
graduating from the Colegio Nacional de Guadalupe, he ma-
triculated in humanities at the University of San Marcos without having a specific career in mind. A gifted and industrious
student, he was named lecturer in philosophy upon completion of his B.A. in 1869. His brilliance and drive astonished
even his mentors when, after receiving his M.A. in 1871, he
went on to obtain his Ph.D. the following year. At this point,
economic insecurity made him turn to law rather than risk a
career in the humanities. Here he also proved to be a superior
student. He earned his J.D. in 1872 and both his LL.M. and
LL.D. in 1873. Fruitful as these two years were in his new
professional field, they were also a source of deep intellectual
frustration for Deústua. Having now completely identified

3. "Deústua y la filosofía de los valores," *Letras*, 13 (1939), 179–80.

himself with the aristocratic, classical ideal of education, he became profoundly disturbed over the prevailing cultural shortcomings among Peru's ruling class. This realization, coupled with his strong civic conscience and his personal commitment to learning, changed the course of Deústua's life. Recognizing the imperative need to educate Peru's social elite, Deústua decided against pursuing a career in law after passing his bar examination in 1875. Instead he chose to continue at the Naval Academy Dos de Mayo in Callao, where he had been assigned by the secretary of education in 1870. He was named head of the Division of Instruction of the Departmental Council and professor of ancient and modern history, philosophy, and geography at the academy in 1877.

On April 5, 1879, Deústua's life took an unexpected turn. The old hostilities over national boundaries between Peru and Chile flared anew, but this time with such unexpected intensity that defiant rhetorical recrimination immediately gave way to overt acts of military belligerency. War between the two nations ensued. At the onset of the War of the Pacific (1879–84), as it was later referred to, the Naval Academy closed its doors. Deústua enlisted, made the rank of second lieutenant, and participated in the disastrous Battle of Miraflores on January 15, 1880.

The War of the Pacific played havoc with Peru, leaving the country vanquished, the spirit of her people extinguished, her populace enveloped by economic ruin. The Peruvians lost not only their social freedom but also their sense of national unity and self-confidence. In this atmosphere of defeat, Deústua dedicated his energies to helping his devastated country recover from the wasting state into which it had fallen. As a politician he accepted the editorship of the Liberal Civilist party's newspaper, *La Opinión Nacional,* and immediately led a blistering attack on the dictatorial policies of Gen. Miguel Iglesias, who had assumed the presidency in Peru with the full backing of Chile. His dauntless criticism helped to prepare the ground for the subsequent civil war in which General Cáceres finally overthrew the Iglesias regime in 1886. In 1901 Deústua was elected senator from Lima, thus stepping from the sidelines into the political limelight. He began his sole term in the forum dramatically by resolving a governmental crisis between President Romaña and Congress. Asked to form a new cabinet, he did so, naming himself secretary of the interior and internal security and retaining that position for the remainder of the congressional session. Having steered Peru out of a trying moment, Deústua retired from active politics in 1904.

Concurrent with his political activities, Deústua also assisted the University of San Marcos in rebuilding the intellectual community during and after the War of the Pacific. To his surprise, he was named adjunct professor of literature and aesthetics even though his theoretical knowledge of aesthetics was limited at the time to the works of Hippolyte Taine, G. W. F. Hegel, and K. C. F. Krause. Considering the appointment honorary, Deústua accepted it, hardly anticipating that his readings in aesthetics, especially those gleaned from Krause, would later change his entire outlook on life and education: "Formaba parte de este escaso alimento estético, la pequeña obra de Krause, en la cual encontré el pensamiento que había de servirme de rumbo en mis futuras investigaciones. En este libro, Krause sostenía que la 'libertad es la esencia de la gracia.' Yo me pregunté si ésa era también la esencia de toda belleza. Mis estudios posteriores . . . me condujeron a concebir y desarrollar una estética fundada en el principio de libertad."[4]

In 1884 Deústua succeeded Dr. Lorente as professor of aesthetics, and in 1902 he was named full professor of philosophy. Among his confreres, it was Deústua who would singly undertake to propagate the ideas of such contemporary philosophers as William James, Wilhelm Wundt, Rudolf Eucken, and, above all, Henri Bergson.[5] Considering himself first and fore-

4. Francisco Miró Quesada, "La filosofía en el Perú actual," *Cursos y Conferencias*, año 13, vol. 25, núm. 149 (1944), 274.

5. Gerhard Masur—"Corrientes filosóficas en América," *Revista de América*, 2 (1945), 134—goes so far as to say that Deústua introduced Bergson to all of South America: "Contra la tendencia práctica y prosaica del positivismo se destaca ahora los valores estéticos y los conceptos de orden y

most a teacher, Deústua, in his modesty, stated that "My best books are my disciples."[6] It will be shown, however, that Deústua's scholarly works stand on their own and single him out as one of the leading philosophers of Latin America in the first quarter of the twentieth century.

In spite of his speculative bent, Deústua was never an absentminded professor. Throughout his professional career he worked assiduously to solve the immediate educational problems facing his country—hence his trips to Argentina (1895) and to Europe (1898–99) to review their public educational systems and to prepare for his later extensive studies on pedagogical reform. Among the latter his most significant monograph was *El problema de la educación nacional.*[7] In 1907 he presented his plan for university reform in "La reforma de exámenes de la Facultad de Letras," a study subsequently published in *Revista Universitaria.*[8] Nationally acclaimed for his accomplishments in the field of pedagogy, Deústua was again commissioned to study the European school systems in 1909, following his secret diplomatic mission before the Holy See in 1908 in which he opposed Chile in

---

libertad en el universo. El pensador peruano Alejandro Deústua refuta las ideas deterministas del positivismo, introduce la filosofía de la evolución creadora en el Perú, y puede decirse en toda la América Latina, donde logra desde los primeros lustros de nuestro siglo influencia considerable." Masur's statement, it should be noted, is debatable. For example, in Mexico, Antonio Caso, although he was not to become a disciple of Bergson until 1914 (when he published his *La filosofía de la intuición*), was familiar with Bergsonian thought by 1910. (See Rosa Krauze de Kolteniuk, *La filosofía de Antonio Caso* [México, 1961], p. 91.) Martin S. Stabb also shows that comments on Bergson, however tangential and shallow, began to appear in Latin America as early as 1907. (See Stabb's *In Quest of Identity: Patterns in the Spanish American Essay of Ideas, 1890–1960* [Chapel Hill, 1967], p. 44, n. 30.)

6. Chiriboga, p. 181.

7. Lima, 1905. This study was subsequently republished in *La cultura nacional*, 2d ed. (Lima, 1937)—hereinafter cited as *CN*—as "El problema pedagógico nacional" (pp. 3–46). (All references to this text are to the *CN* edition and will be incorporated parenthetically in the text. All translations from *CN* are mine.)

8. 1 (1907), 48–52.

the defense of the Peruvian ecclesiastical jurisdiction in the province of Tacna y Arica.

Deústua's second sojourn in Europe (1908–12) led to a fundamental philosophic change in his life. Until then he had followed the worn path of positivism. Together with José Joaquín Mora and Juan Federico Elmore (who introduced the philosophic doctrines of Auguste Comte and Herbert Spencer, respectively), Isaac Alzamora, Mariano H. Cornejo, Manuel Vincente Villarán, and Javier Prado y Ugarteche, Deústua had expounded the theories of evolution and determinism, applying them to Peru's cultural and social reality. While differing with the educational priorities set forth by his colleagues, Deústua had shared their strong faith in scientific knowledge, their belief in progress, and their acceptance of Taine's concept of racial determinism in which environment and moment played a key role in shaping the social state of an age. This naturalistic attitude vanished—although rare positivist regresses occur in Deústua's later writings—during his second stay in Europe. Here, in his early sixties, he experienced a remarkable conversion, embracing the voluntarist psychology of Wundt and the new idealism of Henri Bergson, in whose works he found revitalized Krause's identification of beauty with liberty.

Back in Peru, his trip abroad soon bore fruit. Determined to "combat the reigning intellectualism" in Peru,[9] Deústua published six articles in 1913 in *Revista Universitaria*—"La cultura general y técnica," "Libertad y obediencia," "La escuela de cultura general," "El dualismo en el problema pedagógico," "El deber pedagógico del estado," "Moralidad y educación"[10]—wherein he wedded pedagogy to aesthetics. Championing liberty over order, Deústua turned

9. Miró Quesada, p. 275 (my translation).
10. Respectively, 1, 301–12; 1, 601–14; 2, 232–46; 2, 301–11; 2, 487–500; 2, 551–70. These articles reappeared in 1914 in a monograph entitled *A propósito de un cuestionario sobre la reforma de la ley de instrucción* (Lima). The monograph, in turn, was incorporated in *CN* as "La ley de instrucción" (pp. 267–370).

to art because he was convinced that only through art can man be free. The above studies constituted a natural steppingstone for his next major work, *Las ideas de orden y de libertad en la historia del pensamiento humano*,[11] a philosophic treatise which posited that order and liberty form the very cornerstone of Occidental thought. Stressing that liberty had finally triumphed over order at the dawn of the twentieth century, Deústua concluded by identifying philosophy with aesthetics. Thus Deústua's *Las ideas de orden y de libertad*, in turn, served as an introduction to his *Estética general*. Published in Lima in 1923, *Estética general* systematically embodied Deústua's views on liberty and life. Written at the age of seventy-four, it was undoubtedly his most important contribution to Peruvian thought and marked, moreover, the zenith of Deústua's venture in philosophy.[12]

11. The parts of this work were published in *Revista Universitaria* in the following order: ch. 1, 1 (1917), 1–7; ch. 2, 1 (1917), 7–12; ch. 3, 1 (1917), 12–28; ch. 4, 2 (1917), 300–327; ch. 5, 1 (1918), 139–52; ch. 6, 1 (1918), 429–63; ch. 7, 2 (1918), 40–64; ch. 8, 2 (1918), 379–403; ch. 9, 1 (1919), 173–92; ch. 10, 1 (1919), 321–56; ch. 11, 2 (1919), 3–31; ch. 12, 2 (1919), 269–312; ch. 13, 1 (1920), 3–34; ch. 14, 1 (1920), 277–310; ch. 17, 1 (1922), 79–125; ch. 18, 1 (1922), 126–46; ch. 19, 1 (1922), 147–59. (The last chapter was previously published in *Mercurio Peruano*, 3, 18 [1919], 476–87.) The university strike of 1921 impeded the publication of chapters 15 and 16 in *Revista Universitaria*. The nineteen chapters were later republished in book form: volume 1 (Lima, 1919) contains chapters 1–9; volume 2 (Lima, 1922) contains chapters 10–19. (All subsequent references are to volumes 1 and 2 and will be incorporated parenthetically in the text; translations are mine.)

12. Following his *Estética general*, Deústua published the following three textbooks on aesthetics: *Estética aplicada. Lo bello en la naturaleza* (Lima, 1929); *Estética aplicada. Lo bello en el arte: la arquitectura* (Lima, 1932); and *Estética aplicada. Lo bello en el arte: escultura, pintura y música* (Lima, 1934). (Since these works are only descriptive, they do not fall within the province of this study.) In 1939, Deústua summarized José Vasconcelos's views on aesthetics and rejected them because they are founded on religion in *La estética de José Vasconcelos* (Lima). Deústua's last work—*Los sistemas de moral*, vol. 1 (Lima, 1938) and vol. 2 (Lima, 1940)—is devoid of critical analysis and constitutes a historical survey of the most important ethical systems in Western culture. (All subsequent references to *Estética general* will be incorporated parenthetically in the text; translations are mine.)

# 2. Education, Liberty, and the Creative Man

> What I am really interested in is the new kind
> of education which we must develop which
> moves toward fostering the new kind of human
> being that we need, the process person, the
> creative person, the improvising person, the
> self-trusting, courageous person, the
> autonomous person. It just happens to be a
> historical accident that the art educators are the
> ones who went off in this direction first.
>
> A. H. Maslow
> *The Farther Reaches of Human Nature*

Deústua's preoccupation with pedagogy falls into two distinct
phases. The first was a prolonged gestational but short-lived
positivist stage stretching from 1888 to 1905; it bore but a
single significant, late fruit. The second was an idealistic-
intuitionistic stage that asserted itself after 1909 and constituted the driving force behind Deústua's later extensive philosophical writings. The initial period, strongly influenced by
the writings of August Comte, Herbert Spencer, and Hippolyte Taine, was predominantly down-to-earth in its assess-
ment of the possibility of instituting universal education in
Peru and genetically oriented in its scientific appraisal of
Peruvian society. The idealist stage incorporated the basic
tenets of Bergsonian thought, developing a philosophical con-

9

ception of education, based on the principle of liberty, that
elevates man to the nonrestrictive sphere of aesthetic creation
and frees him from the constraining forces of his national
environment. Deústua's switch from one to the other of these
mutually exclusive philosophical camps was not all that sur-
prising. As a positivist, Deústua was both a pessimist and an
optimist, both a determinist and an altruist. Ultimately, his
unconditional adherence to the latter aspect of positivistic
morality and his unshaken belief in liberty forced him to break
with the prevailing materialistic values professed by his compatriots.

The immediate intellectual climate in which Deústua
found himself did not favor indeterminism. In the years prior
to 1884 there had been little time for gratuitous speculation.
Caught up in anarchy, Peru's primary need was survival. It
was only after the War of the Pacific, when the country found
itself completely prostrated and mutilated, that a methodical
reevaluation of the nation's consciousness became feasible.
Taking up Manuel González Prada's assertion in 1888 that the
regeneration of Peru lay in embracing positive science,[1] Cornejo, Prado y Ugarteche, and Villarán—the most influential
men in Peru at the turn of the century—heralded positivism,
scientific study, and vocational training as the means to save
Peru. Considering racial influence as one of the fundamental
causes of Peru's difficulties, Cornejo maintained that the
present generation had inherited "the lack of self-confidence
of the Indigenous race, a race essentially weak in spirit,
attributable to its fanatic form of government, where supersti-
tion and fanaticism always destroy [man's] character."[2] Prado
y Ugarteche, agreeing with him, urged immigration and the
mixture of races as measures for modifying the Peruvian racial
texture. Excoriating Peru's inadequate educational system,

1. *Páginas libres* (Lima, 1946), p. 46.
2. Quoted by Leopoldo Zea in *Dos etapas del pensamiento en Hispanoamérica* (Mexico, D.F., 1949), p. 242. (The translations from Zea's book
are mine.)

he advocated following the utilitarian American system, which predicated that wealth acquired through diligent work and industry would develop man's character, make him partake in the future of his country, and render him practical and prudent.[3]

Villarán's position was similar. He laid the blame on the Spanish nobility and their representatives in the colonies who attacked "true science, the serious studies which would have awakened progressive ideas," while favoring in their place "the propaganda of theology, scholastic philosophy, Roman jurisprudence, the fine arts, abstract and inoffensive things that could scarcely create any alarm."[4] Addressing himself to his contemporaries, Villarán noted that the high schools did not offer any form of vocational training and that with the exception of the School of Engineering, "not a school of Agriculture nor any [school] of the practical professions" existed at the university level (p. 187). The Peruvian educational system was producing teachers of history, literature, Latin, theology, law, philosophy, and mathematics, "but there is no one who will teach us to farm the land, to raise cattle, to exploit the jungles, to navigate, to trade, to manufacture useful things" (p. 188). In Villarán's mind, the colonial past still dominated Peru. Like Prado y Ugarteche, Villarán also exhorted Peru to follow in the footsteps of the United States by ridding itself of its inherited disdain for work, by abandoning theoretical speculation and adopting a practical attitude toward life. For Villarán, education consisted of instructing the masses: the proletariat and the middle class. The main obligation of the schools was not to produce morally and

3. *Estado social del Perú durante la dominación española (estudio histórico-sociológico)* (Lima, 1894), in *Colección de libros y documentos referentes a la historia del Perú, Tercera serie* (Lima, 1941), pp. 205–6.
4. "Las profesiones liberales en el Perú," from a speech delivered in 1900 at the opening session of the University of San Marcos and subsequently published in *Mercurio Peruano*, 39 (1958), 185. (All references are to this article and will be included parenthetically in the text; the translations are mine.)

aesthetically refined individuals but rather to provide the nation with practical, industrious, and energetic men: "La raza, la tradición, el clima, el territorio, todo nos indica que necesitamos formar hombres prácticos y sensatos, antes que teóricos e imaginativos . . . provistos de potencias y virtudes activas, no de refinamiento morales y estéticos."[5]

In the pedagogical field, at least, it would be erroneous to maintain with Aníbal Sánchez Reulet, Mariano Ibérico, Enrique Barboza, and Julio Chiriboga that Deústua broke with positivism from the outset.[6] As early as 1894 Deústua clearly sympathized with the positivist stand taken by Prado y Ugarteche. Reviewing the latter's book, *Estado social del Perú durante la dominación española*,[7] Deústua defended Prado y Ugarteche—and thereby, tacitly, Villarán and Cornejo—in his thesis of heredity as the determining factor of Peru's malady. Eleven years later, Deústua not only maintained but amplified this point of view in *El problema de la educación nacional*. Although this study broke with Villarán's and Cornejo's prevailing concern over the applied sciences, it did not sever all ties with positivism itself. If Deústua rejected their utilitiarian and technical reforms, it was because they deviated substantially from his own interpretation of Comtian philosophy. Their excessive preoccupation with vocational training indicated that they had identified Comte's scientific age and his concept of progress exclusively with its by-products: wealth and commodities of life. This narrow application of the good was tantamount to turning egotism into a norm of life, an approach which ignored the views of such positivists as Comte, John Stuart Mill, and Spencer, who held that the pursuit of the useful must be superseded by altruism.

5. Quoted by Zea, p. 246.
6. Aníbal Sánchez Reulet, ed., *La filosofía latinoamericana contemporánea* (Washington, D.C., 1949), p. 51; Mariano Ibérico, "La obra filosófica de Don Alejandro O. Deústua," *Letras*, 13 (1939), 147; Barboza, p. 166; and Chiriboga, p. 182.
7. "Un juicio crítico," *El Callao* (Lima), March 28, 1894, reprinted in *Colección de libros y documentos*, pp. 13–25.

For Deústua, economic well-being became morally dissociative when either countries or individuals converted it into their ultimate goal.[8] Because Peru's wealth lay beyond material prosperity, Deústua insisted that the life of his fellow citizens as well as that of his nation be based not on economic weather vanes but rather on philosophical ideals. If Peru was to be saved, she had to establish solid theoretical foundations that would permit the continuation and perfection of her "natural evolution without going astray, without sacrificing the future, without engendering unhappiness . . . " (*CN*, p. 7).

Clearly the pedagogical problem commanded a high priority on Deústua's list of national problems. He argued that it is the most complex and profound of all national problems —involving, as it does, questions of moral, religious, economic, and political interests. Contending that any pedagogical reform must necessarily be based on the particular circumstances of the country, Deústua condemned the prevalent tendency among his compatriots to adopt foreign models without considering their suitability to Peruvian conditions. Notwithstanding his rejection of materialism, however, Deústua did not repudiate practical solutions. He only discarded a priori stands and reforms that are merely "inventions of a fantastic imagination" (*CN*, p. 4).

---

8. This view was vehemently reiterated in 1937 in "Ante el conflicto nacional," *CN*, pp. 137–38: "Pero ninguna tiranía es más desastrosa e inmoral que la derivada de la disciplina económica. El individualismo cuenta con las simpatías del mundo que convierten en un ídolo al becerro de oro y alimenta la corrupción y el servilismo, generadores de toda tiranía. La riqueza, como único valor humano, se impone a los que obedecen como a los que dirigen, dividiendo a la sociedad, no en hombres buenos y malos, sino en ricos y pobres. La seducción de los goces que promete la riqueza disciplina las huestes humanas y las dispone para la guerra en su ambición de monopolizar esos goces, tanto materiales como espirituales. La disciplina económica va hasta erigir el materialismo histórico en la única filosofía positiva, en la única moral y hasta en la única religión. De esa fuente desprende todos los acontecimientos individuales y sociales y crea una nueva Biblia, dentro de la cual se sumergen religión, arte, derecho, política y lógica. El espectáculo desastroso que ofrece la humanidad en estos momentos es obra de la tiranía económica. . . . "

Reviewing the social structure of Peru, Deústua pointed to four conditions responsible for her cultural impoverishment: the bankrupt state of the economy, the moral disintegration of the indigenous population, the frivolous character of the citizenry, and the lack of scientific spirit among the governing class. With respect to the first, reality made it impossible for Peru to respond effectively to the general cry for universal education. Listing the scarcity of teachers, textbooks, and funds as contributing to the failure of elementary education, Deústua maintained that his country's poverty made any thought of organizing a primary cycle outside the capital itself inconceivable. Thus, even over a period of years, the influences of primary education on the population would be negligible at best. Inverting the materialistic arguments of his contemporaries that schools necessarily stimulate work and thus foster morality, Deústua went on to assert, as did Comte, that any desirable and permanent social improvement must be preceded by an appropriate moral transformation. Only a solid moral foundation can generate fruitful work; work, stripped of its moral fiber, in and by itself, would lead only to social and spiritual disintegration.

Furthermore, Deústua asserted that the influence of primary education in Peru was negligible, because the inhabitants of *puñas* and *caseríos*, who should have benefited most from such a project, are inherently incapable of improvement.[9] They were, in Deústua's aristocratic eyes, a people of exceptional "meekness," living at a moral level

9. In "Ante el conflicto nacional," Deústua reasserted that the Indians had reached their maximum evolutionary development and possessed "all the energy of inertial matter in order to conserve itself in that cycle and not enter fully, as a factor of life, in the movement of superior races. . ." (*CN*, p. 60). The effects of alcohol and coca consumption had been transmitted "from generation to generation, producing abnormal human beings" (*CN*, p. 67). Psychologically, the Indian had inherited feelings of hate, fear, hypocrisy, and an instinctual aversion to civilization. His moral resurrection was possible, Deústua emphasized, only if "psychic forces strong enough

which only provoked pity. He attributed their docility either to ingrained psychological factors rooted in their unconscious state or to their sheer resignation, pounded in by centuries of submission until it had become an innate part of their character. Expressing bigoted views that will always haunt and mar the work of an otherwise exemplary herald of human liberty and dignity, Deústua declared that they lacked both spiritual refinement and interest in acquiring knowledge. He held that they were human only in "form," lacking that feeling of human dignity essential to a culture. There was no reason to suppose that their happiness lay in knowing history or geography, subjects of little relevance to their daily lives, pursued under abject poverty. "Only an intellectualist outlook of civilization," Deústua stated," can conceive of happiness under those conditions" (*CN*, p. 14). Thus—contrary to Comte, who believed that universal education formed the very foundation of the new positivist social order—Deústua adamantly maintained that in Peru there was no point in being preoccupied with popular education. In this respect, Deústua relied heavily on Spencer's theory of evolution and dissolution, believing that the Indian and mestizo were in a state of dissolution or disorganization that rendered their moral progress impossible. Thus to deplete Peru's treasury in this educational adventure would serve no purpose. Rather, practicality demanded that efforts be undertaken to correct the social backwardness of this group. Above all, their most essential needs had to be met: freedom from the tyranny of their overseers, hygienic living conditions, and instruction in the

---

to warrant such a rebirth exist in a virtual state in the subconscious nature of the Indian." Deústua, it should be noted, totally rejected this possibility: "The poor conscious base of the Indian prior to the conquest does not suggest any idea whatsoever of free force, endowed with that spontaneity that the redeeming conversion demands" (*CN*, p. 67). In fact, Deústua's deterministic bias was so extreme that he denied any hope of redemption for the Indian: "In our opinion the servitude of the Indian conscious is irredeemable" (*CN*, p. 68).

technical skills necessary to farm their lands profitably. Only through such corrective measures could one ultimately hope to humanize them and make them content. Yet such an enterprise, Deústua desperately confessed, was beyond the country's present capability: "¡Pero, cuánto tiempo y cuánto dinero y cuánto esfuerzo se necesita para esa labor! Abruma el calcularlo. Somos todavía muy pobres para llevar a cabo esa misión civilizadora, que grandes naciones apenas han podido iniciar" (CN, p.14).

The great indigenous and mestizo populations, however, were not the sole cause of the "inequities" suffered by Peru. Nor for that matter were they totally responsible for the regressive character of the Peruvian collective life. Deústua attributed the nation's impoverishment to the basic "inertia" of the composite mixture of her races (CN, p. 4), to her inability to overcome "the old traditions [Indian and colonial] of the race" (CN, p. 19).[10] Driven by the unyielding "egoism of the [Peruvian] race" (CN, p. 19), the people's inherited,

10. In his speech "La crisis política," delivered on March 19, 1914, and subsequently published in CN, Deústua's position toward Spain resembled Villarán's. Reviewing his country's history, Deústua found Peru submerged in an atmosphere of skepticism. Her actual decadent state was not the result of immediate and transitory problems; rather, her defeat and bankruptcy could be traced to a single cause which resided in the origin of her civilization. The settlement of Peru had been based completely on an economic foundation, stressing the rapid acquisition of personal wealth. Spain, enriching its coffers, had infused a utilitarian morality into its colonies. Even after Peru became independent, Spain's influence persisted. The new political leaders shared the same cultural background as the former colonial government and continued their policies. Material goals, immoral in Deústua's eyes, continued to dominate now-independent Peru because her national conscience was too feeble to overcome or radically change the old ingrown political patterns. The country merely succumbed to economic interests and sacrificed inventive future projects for immediate concrete benefits (CN, pp. 40–50). After the War of the Pacific, Peruvian leaders were convinced that happiness, power, and liberty depended exclusively on the "quantitative growth of the nation" (CN, p. 8), which manifested itself in the cult of luxury and in the formation of strong armed forces. They failed to perceive that the "shining clothes" concealed "dissociative forces" (CN, p. 8). The results of this policy were disastrous. It made moral cripples of Peru's citizens, who believed in the "omnipotence of

materialistic spirit nullified all attempts to stabilize the nation, permitting anarchy to prevail.[11] Yet social anarchy was nothing more than an effect of the anarchical tendencies that stemmed from the "anarchy of the biological and psychological forces of the individual derived from the mingling of antagonistic races . . . " (*CN*, p. 23). Peru's past continued to infuse her present. The pernicious influence of the social milieu, shrouded in an atmosphere of amoral materialism, foreshadowed in turn an ominous future: "Vivimos así encadenados por una necesidad de transigir con el mal, sin poder salir de esa esclavitud, porque las nuevas generaciones siguen el ejemplo de las anteriores y los nuevos gobiernos no encuentran otro camino viable que el recorrido por sus antecesores. No se suscitan nuevos gérmenes, ni se corrigen oportunamente los que nacen a la vida con la herencia viciosa de nuestra raza" (*CN*, p. 6). And in a later passage (wherein the influence of Taine is very visible) he stated: "Tenemos el impulso destructor en las entrañas y cedemos, por falta de educación, a ese impulso, movidos por esta naturaleza enfermiza, que el mestizaje, la herencia y el medio han formado, perpetuando, sin oposición, un estado anormal del que no nos damos cuenta . . . " (*CN*, p. 23).

In such an atmosphere, progress was impossible. What Peru lacked was moral guidance—in short, education among its ruling class. Deústua insisted, as Robert Maynar Hutchins did forty years later in the United States, on building from the top down. The country's greatest need was for a disin-

---

money, even [in its power] to buy off morality" (*CN*, p. 8), and who valued man as if he were a social machine. Deústua's condemnation was as virulent as it was brief: "Hemos sido ricos y derrochadores y sentimos la nostalgia de placeres corruptores, adquiridos fácilmente y sin medida" (*CN*, p. 8).

11. A quarter of a century later, Deústua reviewed the political evolution of his country in "Ante el conflicto nacional" and concluded that it had come to a halt. Worse still, he believed Peru to be in the initial stage of "repetitive evolution" of her "political life." Together, the two constitute anarchy. Hence, Deústua saw anarchy as the first movement of a nation which, condemned to stagnation, does not die but rather keeps on transforming without ever renovating itself (*CN*, p. 103).

terested intellectual aristocracy—a society based on aristocratic
values. At a time when psychological change might have been
possible—after the War of the Pacific—the absence of an intellectual elite only drove Peru deeper into stagnation.[12] Anticipating Ortega y Gasset's famous essay "The Revolt of the Masses"
(1930), Deústua perceived that the ruling class had abandoned
their responsibility of leadership and had joined the ranks of the
masses. In an attempt to restore the national spirit, Deústua
exhorted the political leaders to act, to brush aside their illusions, to face up to reality. His appeal stressed moral qualities
above logical, economic, and—most interestingly, considering
his about-face in his later writings—aesthetic criteria: "Es preciso valorizar a los hombres por lo bueno que hacen y no por lo
bello que dicen o que exhiben o por sus condiciones de audacia.
Es preciso colocar el criterio moral sobre el criterio lógico, estético y económico . . . " (CN, p. 25). As a firm disciple of positivism, Deústua also underlined the scientific cause: ". . . y vol-
teando la espalda al viejo espíritu nacional . . . hagamos obra de
educación con el auxilio de la ciencia, disciplinando las inteli-
gencias con los métodos científicos modernos y reformando las
voluntades para echar las raíces de la paz y la armonía desde el
comienzo mismo de la vida consciente" (CN, pp. 25–26). In fact,
morality and science were seen to be intimately fused—a view
which he repudiated after 1913—since direct and unbiased ob-
servations of natural and human phenomena not only correct
man's atavistic behavioral impulses but also free him from egotistical interests creating an unprejudiced vision of life.

Besides science, Deústua called upon two other dis-
ciplines, history and philosophy, to arouse Peru from its
lethargy. He bid history to criticize current events severely and
impartially, neither inventing nor sugarcoating them for political reasons. The nation's sad past had to be exhibited in

12. History has proven, Deústua contended in "La ley de instrucción," that progress is achieved by a selected minority: ". . . progress has
always been the work of an initial few which has been imposed on the
masses oftentimes after bloody sacrifices" (CN, p. 349).

its nakedness in order to persuade the ruling class of the folly of elaborating programs based on myths. In contrast to history's single role, Deústua gave philosophy two educational tasks: to dissipate traditional errors held as epistemological postulates "of conscious phenomena" (*CN*, p. 27) and, in a more positive vein, to replace false assumptions with new truths. Deústua was certain that the latter, in particular, would ultimately have repercussions in the social sciences. He predicted that the new truths established by reason would engender political reform and influence the nation as a whole; through the observation and study of man, the discipline of philosophy would direct his countrymen toward the path "least exposed to the unbalanced mental conditions which beget the misfortunes of humanity" (*CN*, p. 27). What Peru needed was a philosophy capable of formulating a doctrine based on the data of scientific sociology, emphasizing that human life is at the same time a "product" as well as an "agent." Contradicting his former prejudiced and deterministic view of the Indian, Deústua added (although it is unlikely that he was thinking of the Indian when he made these remarks) that "happiness is not the exclusive result of the rigorous determinism of biological laws . . . " (*CN*, p. 28). Deústua affirmed that man's power is limitless in what it can do to change nature. To triumph, man must discard the notion that strife and harmony are mutually exclusive absolutes. Rather, both are relative factors "that intermingle in the evolutionary process of civilization . . ." (*CN*, p. 28).[13]

13. In "La crisis política," Deústua considered evolution as a spontaneous, natural process "that passes from one instance to the next in life without the possibility of a regressive movement into the past" (*CN*, p. 57). Within this process, Deústua stated in "Ante el conflicto nacional," the human conscious, propelled by a "free force," shatters, "without obeying any logic whatsoever, the hard shell formed by traditional activity . . . " (*CN*, p. 83). However, if such a concept is valid, it must be universally so; that is, it must also apply to the Indian. Deústua's failure to recognize this in 1905 has already been noted. Lamentably, Deústua denied the spontaneous character of evolution to the Indian in "Ante el conflicto nacional," and categorically rejected the idea of an "indefinite progress of individual consciousness" (*CN*, p. 68). His insistence on man's limited psychological

20 Alejandro O. Deústua

Taking into consideration Deústua's remarks, it is evident that in 1905 he harbored no illusions of finding rapid solutions to Peru's problems. Indeed, as long as there existed "the hope of a favorable evolution determined by an education adequate to our nature" (*CN*, p. 31), radical changes were impossible. The nation had to be satisfied with taking a few but firm steps. The implantation of new moral values had to be undertaken gradually, and only after sufficient social preparation, so that the modification of Peru's nationality did not strip the country of its psychological autonomy. Before Peru could build, it had to critically demolish the old spirit and tear itself away from the enveloping foreign influences retained by the "plasticity of the national race" (*CN*, p. 31) and unresisted by the inertia of the governing class. For Deústua, Peru's salvation did not lie in the collective will or in the mythical resurrection of the primitive energies of the masses but rather in the "scientific creation of a new existence" (*CN*, p. 39) directed, as Comte would have it, by an intellectual elite.[14] As such a group of dedicated public servants could only be formed at institutions of higher learning, Deústua charged

---

development shows that even as late as 1937 some vestiges of his old positivist heritage had not altogether disappeared: "En nuestro concepto la esclavitud de la conciencia en el indio es irremediable. Nosotros no creemos en el progreso indefinido de la conciencia individual. Nos parece más acertada la hipótesis de que cada individuo, cada raza, adquiere una intensidad limitada en su energía síquica que desenvuelve, sin pasar de ese límite, en las diversas etapas de su historia. Lo que pasa en el hombre individual se repite en la sociedad [and here remnants of Saint-Simon, Comte, and Spencer can be seen], aún cuando no sea muy exacto hablar de infancia, juventud y vejez en la historia de los pueblos. De allí que hay razas que sobreviven a los desastres de sus fuerzas anímicas y reaccionan poderosamente con las fuerzas conservadas en sus raíces; mientras que otras sucumben pasando de un vigoroso dinamismo a un estatismo irremediable" (*CN*, p. 68).

14. Deústua, like Comte, was also attacked for his intellectual position. In his book *7 ensayos de interpretación de la realidad peruana*, 2d ed. (Lima, 1943), José Carlos Mariátegui assailed Deústua's views on education as antidemocratic and antisocial. Deústua stood for "the old aristocratic mentality of the latifundiary caste" (p. 114; my translation).

the university, and not the primary or secondary institutions, with the education of future leaders. He was confident that the university would produce a disinterested ruling class ready to sacrifice its own egotistical interests for that of the public good. The university would create, in short, social solidarity essential to real government.[15] A natural optimist, Deústua had faith that education invited truth and that truth would assure the advent of liberty.

The above emphasis on liberty is of capital importance since it separated Deústua from his fellow Peruvian positivists in 1905 and explained his rejection of positivism after 1913. His stress on liberty can be traced to two sources. The first is immediate and refers to Deústua's view of science as a totally disinterested discipline; the second is mediate and goes back to Krause's comment that liberty and beauty are intimately bound together. Of the two, the latter must be considered the original source, inasmuch as it explains the former. Otherwise, the still prevailing eighteenth-century mechanistic conception of science in Peru—Deústua was, after all, a determinist much like Comte, Spencer, and Taine—would have indubitably eliminated the term *liberty* from Deústua's work in 1905. The basic concept gleaned from Krause in 1882 was a seed firmly implanted in Deústua's mind that unconsciously drove him to reject absolute necessity at the very end.

The awakening occurred during Deústua's second stay on the Continent between 1908 and 1912. At the age of sixty, his unusual intellectual resiliency allowed him to recognize the

15. Eight years later this intellectual, aristocratic conception reappeared, more pronounced. In "El deber pedagógico del estado," Deústua alleged that the university forms the true state because it alone "offers the instruments of social organization without which the State could not be a political reality . . . (*CN*, p. 351). The university, with its "liberal arts" ("cultura general") curriculum, inculcates social solidarity and creates a nation out of the state by generating high moral standards, implanting an ethics of abnegation, encouraging individual initiative, and proclaiming liberty as the sacred tenet of life. In short, Deústua maintained that " 'to educate' is 'to govern' " (*CN*, p. 351).

extraordinary vitality of a new idealism which was completely in tune with his own deeply rooted elitist Weltanschauung. Subsequent readings of Bergson, the apologist of life, and of Wundt prompted Deústua to sever his ties with positivist morality and to embrace the cause of indeterminism. Consequently, Deústua's restatement of his aristocratic ideas in 1913 appeared in an altogether different light than in 1905. Under the aegis of Bergson, Deústua now stressed culture and an aesthetic approach to life. He asserted that the spirit is creativity, a force of inner concentration which vitalizes the external world. This inevitably led him to condemn the cause-and-effect method of science and to renounce reason. He argued, in his defense of life, that both science and reason freeze the objective as well as the subjective worlds into inert micro clots. Man cannot turn to reason and science, therefore, to probe and understand the flowing secrets of reality. To do so, he must turn to intuition—that is, he must avail himself of his aesthetic faculty, the faculty of liberty itself.

Upon his return to Peru, Deústua's dissatisfaction with antiquated positivist postulates induced him to strike out aggressively against scientism in his country. Taking the positivists head-on, he systematically assailed them from three successive directions: pedagogy, philosophy, and aesthetics. (The three, it should be noted, are intimately related in that they expound a unitary concept of life.) The first attack came in 1913 in six articles,[16] commonly referred to in Peru as "La ley de instrucción" (the title under which they were republished in *La cultura nacional*); it reflected a vitalist approach to education. In "La ley de instrucción" Deústua averred that pedagogy must depart from the subjective and objective experience of life if it wants to determine the ideal norm of conduct, if it desires to deal with man's destiny, and if it wishes to clarify the relationship between individual and social happiness. Without this basic psychological and sociologi-

16. See ch. 1, n. 10.

cal knowledge of the concrete man, the efforts undertaken by pedagogy would produce sterile results. Concerned with life itself, with the expansion of man's spirit, Deústua refused to have any preconceived "definitive plan" (*CN*, p. 276) imposed upon education. Rigidity narrowed the horizons of appreciation with its assembly-line production of a single type of human being: rote men made for a rote nation. What Peru needed was an educational system based on flexibility, a system that stressed individuality, creativity—in short, an approach to pedagogy that acknowledged life not as stasis but as duration: ". . . la vida es un 'devenir' . . . una melodía infinita cuyos temas, siempre nuevos, se suscitan recíprocamente en el curso del ritmo universal, sin poderse encerrar jamás en un cuadro completo, preconcebido, a la manera del viejo finalismo que petrificaba los contornos de la realidad vivida . . . " (*CN*, p. 276).

This outlook unequivocally eliminated the possibility of adopting what were then the two prevailing pedagogical tendencies in Peru: the scientific or positivist stand and the traditional Catholic view. In a complete about-face from the beliefs he had expressed in 1905, Deústua denounced the spiritual consequences of a scientific culture. The notion of science for science's sake rang false and empty. In contrast to his previous position, Deústua no longer divorced science from technical and material progress. The two—the theoretical and the practical—were "inseparable in experiential reality" (*CN*, p. 297). Without its practical effects, science "would be of little consequence . . . " (*CN*, p. 297). Accordingly, Deústua was fully aware that a society based on scientific ideals could only engender a culture whose grounds for happiness depended on material well-being; he maintained that this was precisely what had occurred during his era. The prodigious development of material wealth stemming from scientific progress had produced a society that flatly proclaimed "the economic person . . . as the most perfect type of man" (*CN*, p. 304). Indifferent, science had cast society to the rigors of determinism, anchoring life—thought of by Deústua as a free, expanding, spiritual force—to supreme natural laws. On the practical level, it had failed to create the moral man because science was indifferent to the ethical implications of its discoveries. Having obtained overwhelming support for the development of vocational and technical schools, science had taken education down the path of mercantilism, leaving behind a society bound by egotistical bonds. Since utilitarian interests could rear only suspicion and not confidence among the members of society, social solidarity, the primary goal of education and of society itself, could hardly be procured when a nation remained content to pay homage to scientific culture.

Catholicism, Deústua admitted, served as a buffer to absorb the impact of positivism in Peru. Although he appreciated this important counterbalancing effect of religion, he was fully cognizant of its shortcomings as the governing principle of education. Religion served as an adequate antidote to science by emancipating man from his utilitarian drive. Advocating inner—that is, spiritual—concentration, Catholicism eradicated science's pleasure principle of material indulgence and replaced it with the notion of self-sacrifice and the mystical desire to cut all ties with the material world. Yet, by submerging the conscious into "the inner recess of that divine Ideal Power, whose will, as an absolute norm, invades the entire [human] conscious . . . " (CN, p. 336), religion in effect deprived the individual of his liberty and annihilated man's autonomy. To exchange science for religion amounted to trading one deterministic perspective for another. Just as science had endeavored to reduce man to nature's rigorous laws—to make him follow nature and believe in her laws—so had religion tried to lure man to accept the ideas of a divine intelligence as the sole creator and director of phenomena. It had subjugated physical order to a divine one. Not only did God create and direct external phenomena, He also ordered and prescribed that man render absolute obedience to Him. Deústua consequently rejected religion as the foundation of culture. Ultimately, it bred intolerance and dogmatism because it created a "false idea of human values . . . " (*CN*, p. 281) and, above all, because it established social solidarity not in but outside of the individual himself: " . . . the free solidarity of souls cannot spring from bonds placed outside the conscious . . . " (*CN*, p. 305).

Confronted by these two opposites, Deústua straddled the difficulty by adopting an idealistic position which reconciled both tendencies and formed the moral character of man at the same time. Man, his individual existence and his relationship to society, was foremost in Deústua's mind. His task lay in discovering a transcendental and eternal principle which would serve as the foundation of social solidarity. Deústua affirmed that this primordial principle is liberty: "the essence of all life and of all spirit" (*CN*, p. 283). Solidarity, in turn, suggests the notions of liberty and order—concepts which, it is important to note, Deústua further developed in 1917 in order to establish the philosophical basis of his aesthetics. As both liberty and order are expressions of the dual character of life—of its subjective and objective elements, respectively—both are necessary to the process of culture. Deústua referred to liberty without order as "explosive"; it becomes a force which would waste its energy in "unsuccessful attempts of evolution . . . " (*CN*, p. 301). He recognized that new elements must be introduced under some form of order if liberty is to exist. Describing order as the negation of time, of change—that is to say, of life itself—Deústua could not admit it as an end of moral education. He was willing to admit that order emerges as a logical necessity imposing itself upon life, which he identified with consciousness. But he insisted that order is always subservient to liberty: "La vida y la conciencia son libertad, fuerza expansiva que atiende a la armonía por esa simpatía intelectual, que engendra la solidaridad del movimiento del espíritu con la inercia de la materia, a la que domina, penetra y vivifica" (*CN*, p. 293). An integral concept of culture, then, must embrace the two activities pertaining to cognition: logic and intuition. The first searches for order and results in the creation of science, while the second leads to the knowledge "of free life" (*de la vida libre*) and begets art, religion, and philosophy (*CN*, p. 303). Without their presence, then, morality and culture would lack both depth and breadth: "Sin la concurrencia de ambas funciones la moralidad es imposible y la cultura se desorienta y produce un desarrollo unilateral del hombre, de funestas consecuencias" (*CN*, p. 303).

Deústua could therefore accept science as a useful tool: the domination of matter would allow the human spirit, that is, life, to expand freely and to fulfill itself. Nevertheless, this left him with the problem of eradicating egotism, a feeling that was, on the one hand, instinctual (that is, prespiritual) and, on the other, a scientific residual of affluency. Here religion could play out its vital role by emancipating man from egotism. Deústua readily accepted this benefit afforded by religion, but he saw the subordination of man and his will to an external omnipotent being as reducing morality to the state of "pure obligation" (*CN*, p. 281). If morality were to exist at all, Deústua ardently insisted, it would have to be based on the principle of liberty, the only unconditional imperative of morality.

In other words, morality was an outcome, not a creator, of liberty. It was not the creator of ethical ideals; rather, it only imposed the norms created by another discipline. The same held true for pedagogy. Pedagogy established its canons of education and discipline keeping in view the development of the ideal man. But the ideal man was given to, not begotten by, pedagogy. This meant that, for Deústua, man acquired morality in and by an act of freedom and that the penetration or knowledge of this reality was a prerequisite to the act of liberty itself.

From all these considerations, Deústua inferred that neither reason (science's instrument for understanding external reality and reducing it to order and determinism) nor materialism (providing, at best, egotistical bonds of momentary solidarity) could lead man to morality. The perception of liberty, that inner reality, was feasible simply through intuition. And since intuition was the very basis, the starting point, of art, Deústua unhesitatingly conceded to the aesthetic faculty the sole power capable of forging and preserving a truly free inner life. In this respect, then, Deústua differed radically from many other philosophers who have linked pedagogy to art. Whereas they considered art essentially in a didactic light, serving higher causes or ideals outside of man, Deústua would have pedagogy deliver the profound Self of an individual through art.[17] To be creative is to be free; consciousness, in its psychic creativity, denotes inner liberation.

17. The idea that art is tied to pedagogy is not new. It reaches back to the first moments when philosophers began to speculate on art and its place in society. The following are a few examples of philosophic reflection on art and pedagogy from ancient Greece to the present time. Plato would have had the artist awaken and instill in the citizens those emotions thought to be useful to the state. Aristotle, taking self-realization and self-fulfillment as a basic tenet, maintained that art should present life as it "ought" to be in order to better the nature of man so that he might imitate the good life. The Stoics did not separate beauty from the moral good and sought to portray human dignity (decorum) through the beautiful. Horace believed that art's function is to instruct and to delight, to record virtuous acts, and to correct social passions and evils.

In turn, the Church—through the Church Fathers—assumed complete sovereignty over man's mind and used art to propagate its religious teachings. Boileau, influenced by Descartes, declared that the function of art is to disclose nature's truth in clear and distinct ideas. Hegel wanted art to become a vessel of the Idea and of the State, the sole sovereign entity in society. Even Schiller, for whom freedom played an essential role in aesthetics, thought that artistic work should serve as a corrective to man's excessive sexuality, rudeness, frivolity, and caprice. David wanted the artist to use his art to impart civic virtue, heroism, patriotic fervor, and the love of glory. Comte, like Hegel, conceived art as a vehicle for social and political designs dictated by the positive State, but—and here he differed from Hegel—he wanted the artist to idealize reality and lead man to a state of perfection. This idea of instructing and saving mankind, that every poet must possess a mission, and that art is most beautiful when it places itself at the service of progress was best exemplified in the person of Victor Hugo. Similarly, Proudhon held that the artist had to fulfill a social cause, namely, that of exalting human dignity. Tolstoy, the main spokesman of art as the communication of emotion, also imparted to the artist the task of diffusing the Christian feelings of love and brotherhood. After World War I, the surrealist movement became a springboard for political propaganda. In the 1930s, totalitarian states such as Italy, Germany, and Russia all employed art to further their political ideology, a phenomenon which also occurs in countries presently under fascist and communist rule.

Rendered in concrete terms, creative consciousness is expressed in art. With the aid of art, man relaxes his hold on his habit-worn survival guard and learns to esteem an impractical percept of qualities, learns to value the expression of a disinterested moment of dynamic and vital originality. Hence, consciousness and art go hand in hand. Through art, the artist's personality, his conscious, unfurls its manifest penetration and immersion into the interiority of reality and reveals them to another receptive conscious. The artistic creation, a unique object of its kind, is a totally gratuitous act of communication from one Self that endures to another. The artistic product, as a result, must be considered an unadulterated act of true social solidarity. Hence, art becomes education and constitutes its most prized instrument to bring out and expand the inner liberty that is man. Like art, the aesthetic education of man promotes habit-breaking, not habit-forming, acts. Art, and art alone, makes man autonomous. Like consciousness and art, art and pedagogy must also go hand in hand.

> La Moral no crea normas, que son ideales de vida, sino que las impone con fuerza coercitiva y absoluta después de creados por la imaginacíon artística. La Pedagogía no establece sus cánones de educación y de disciplina, sino en vista de un hombre ideal, que toma como modelo del hombre del porvenir, del hombre perfecto. La Pedagogía no crea ese tipo: es el Arte el que lo crea; porque solo el Arte crea tipos o ideales penetrados de vida, capaces de servir de modelos, a diferencia de las categorías lógicas aplicables a los conceptos puros. [CN, p. 345]

# 3. The Philosophic Dilemma: Order and Liberty

In general—history and one's personal
experience confirm this—the instinct of
conservation obliges one to affirm life in spite of
the pain, in spite of the condemnation that it
deserves from us during the bitter hours. Nor
does the pessimistic denial save us from action.
We have no other alternative but to choose a
side in the contest. We can do without
theories, action always imposes itself [upon us].
"At the beginning there was action." Not at the
beginning of things, but at the beginning of
human redemption. Through action the species
has forged its culture, technique, human and
spiritual; through culture it pursues its
emancipation from all servitude. Culture is the
work of the will; the will desires liberty. Let it
be *creative liberty.*

Alejandro Korn, *Philosophical Notes*

The fusion in 1913 of pedagogy and aesthetics played a decisive role in Deústua's subsequent philosophic and aesthetic
inquiries. Asserting that creation, art, imaginative activity—
in short, inner liberty—mark the new criteria of contemporary philosophy, Deústua renewed his attack on positivism in
1914. Scrutinizing Occidental thought in search of a pattern

29

that would substantiate his particular Weltanschauung, Deústua found a pendular design for the role played by order and liberty in philosophy. This contrasts sharply with Auguste Comte's positivist evolutionary perspective. Comte spoke of the continuous progress of human intelligence and never adverted to the psychological act of volition—that is, inner liberty. Indeed, Comte negated the very possibility of liberty because he perceived nothing outside of determinism: " . . . true liberty is nothing else than a rational submission to predominance of the laws of nature [which are rigorous and invariable], in release from all arbitrary personal dictation."[1]

Clearly, then, Deústua's pedagogical ideas after 1912 constituted an initial attack on the Comtian citadel of material progress. The amelioration of a people, Deústua averred, comes not through matter but through the soul—a point which Deústua, in his meticulous analysis of Western philosophy, repeatedly emphasized. Might this not imply, then, that one of Deústua's underlying (but undeclared) purposes in embarking on his new study was to counteract and shatter the pernicious misconceptions promulgated by Joaquín de Mora and José Antonio Barrenechea, who held that only a technocratic society could save Peru? If Deústua could show that civilization had continuously fluctuated between order and liberty, that these two concepts formed the cornerstone of humanity's spiritual journey through time,[2] would this not, in effect, raze Comte's theory of necessary and indefinite progress in set stages and destroy the belief that the industrial stage constituted the pinnacle of human progress? And would this not prove that Peru's salvation need not lie in a society enslaved and dedicated to economic well-being? Deústua was convinced that positivism erred in its belief that technology and industry inevitably brought about altruism and affective progress. (We recall that even in his early

1. *Positive philosophy*, trans. Harriet Martineau, 3 vols. (London, 1896), bk. 6, ch. 1. (All subsequent references to books and chapters are to this edition and are incorporated parenthetically in the text.)
2. Francisco Miró Quesada, "La filosofía del orden y de la libertad y su influencia práctica," *Letras*, no. 13 (1939), 196.

positivist period, Deústua sought truth through science to generate liberty and not to further material progress.) Peru stood as an example that social solidarity did not evolve by means of industrialization. The application of positive polity in Peru repressed right—Comte's social utopia would substitute *duty* (altruism) for *right*—and ensured the prolongation of political turmoil, economic disarray, and social havoc. Furthermore, Deústua foresaw that this new Peruvian order, if left unfettered, would inevitably deploy the arts to depict a living and appealing representation of future society conforming to the sanctioned positive demarcations of human magnificence and reverence to matter. For Deústua, the aims of a positive state logically purported the total annihilation of man and denied him the liberty to formulate his conscious. Comte himself had stated unequivocally (bk. 6, ch. 1) that the unbound liberty of the mind could never be considered "an organic principle" and, moreover, constituted a serious impediment to the reorganization of society in a positive state.

Deústua's personal commitment to liberty, coupled with his review of a positive state, made the study on order and liberty that much more imperative. While to champion the cause of liberty was, in effect, to save Peru, in a larger context his study soared above national frontiers. It looked to man and exalted man's creative talents, identifying liberty with artistic expression. The treatise on order and liberty, therefore, could only be undertaken on a theoretical plane, owing to the fact that in the last analysis Deústua considered his work an introduction to aesthetics itself: "Este estudio sirve de introducción al desarrollo histórico de las ideas estéticas que ofrecen una tentativa de conciliación entre esos dos conceptos característicos de la belleza: el de orden y el de la libertad" (1, 3). Such then, is the genesis of Deústua's lengthy philosophical treatise *Las ideas de orden y de libertad en la historia del pensamiento humano.* [3]

3. 2 vols. (Lima: Casa Editora Ernesto R. Villarán, 1919–22). The above and subsequent volume and page citations in this chapter are references to this edition and are included parenthetically in the text.

Deústua was convinced that the concepts of order and liberty form the nucleus of all philosophical systems in the history of ideas: dominating alternately in the evolution of human thought, they are nonexclusive concepts, opposite but not contradictory, that tend toward different yet conciliatory ends. Order springs from man's cognitive activities, while liberty is the expression of psychic life that aspires to expand free of restraint. Intimately related to such notions as space-duration, substance-phenomenon, state-change, and unity-plurality, they find their basic expression in the concepts of necessity and contingency. The above antipodal ideas have their origin in a common teleological function, namely, to render nature intelligible through the systematization of her phenomena, reducing the latter to the categories of thought.

According to Deústua, a strong spontaneous tendency of the spirit impels man to explain the perpetual becoming of phenomena under the principle of unity. Multiplicity, diversity, and movement are thereby excluded, and free will, proscribed. For Deústua it is this human need to perceive things in a unified manner that leads to the idea of genus and to the concepts of force, substance, the absolute, and universal law. While the elimination of differences and the synthesis of similarities—that is, the transformation of concrete perceptions into concepts—have produced the notion of pure unity, the reverse tendency has always guided man back to the individual, which, for Deústua, is inseparable from the idea of liberty. Of the two, necessity (order, unity) is a purely logical and thereby an ideal systematization, whereas contingency (liberty) is a reality that cannot be systematized. Consequently, Deústua speculated that the philosophical idea of necessity has its origin in mathematics, logic, and astronomy, where things cannot appear but in a precise, rigorous, and immutable manner. In turn, the idea of contingency or unpredictability arises from the observation of the unlimited diversity of biological phenomena and, above all, of moral phenomena which can take place outside of a preestablished order. In short, for Deústua order and liberty constitute two facets of human activity, one ideal, the other real. The first is extraneous to life and movement; the second, in its process of incessant creation, is one with life and movement. They have always coexisted in the progress of human thought, although liberty, or life, for the most part has found itself under the constant vigil and domination of order—that is, "the rational principle" ("el pensamiento ordenador") (1, 5).

As Deústua saw it, the necessary condition for liberty at the outset of human existence consists in the domination of the external world through order; without this order, the awakening and development of the expansive tendency of the spirit could not take place. At this stage of human development, reason, incapable of abstracting forms and engendering pure concepts, gives rise to cosmogonies and theologies. The imagination of primitive man imposed order by ascribing human attributes to nature and left all external phenomena dependent on an intelligence and will similar to his own. Simultaneous phenomena then appeared to him to form systems; and these, in turn, became means by which he could aspire to obtain and exalt a unique and supreme end. The universe was converted into a unique system composed of inferior systems, in themselves composed of other systems, and so on successively. Each phenomenon had a specific end within its own particular whole and each particular whole played a specific, determined, orderly role within the totality of things. Thus, everything necessarily partook in the beautiful order of the universe. This primitive vision, this primitive interpretation, begot mythology. Once purified of its naïveté, it led to the creation in Asia and Asia Minor of the diverse religions in which the universal and organizing principle of the elements of nature appeared under the form of a supreme intelligence. The apparent chaos of the external world, chaos which at first impressed the primitive mind as the eternal matter, thus slowly took on a fixed, orderly pattern and confined the scope of the contingent and the unexpected which had been identified up to that point with liberty. Order, perceived as the governing law of phenomena, now prevailed and bridled imagination and intuition.

Of all the ancient civilizations, Deústua was particularly drawn to that of Greece, because of its intrinsic magnificence and its continuous influence on Occidental culture. In Greece, he pointed out, the gods made their entrance on the human stage as cosmic legislators and as distributors of life. A specific law governed each being in nature, and from the harmonious agreement of these living laws arose the divine, eternal, and beautiful symphony of the universe which the Greeks called the cosmos. Although religion undoubtedly played an important role in Hellenic culture, Deústua maintained that it never inhibited the Greek mind. The Greeks were forever intellectualizing about the phenomena of the external world, even to the point of threatening to destroy their own religious creations. Slowly the poetic, mythological interpretations of the cosmos gave way to philosophical interpretations of phenomena, as the mind relentlessly strove to discover the first cause of the universe.

It was precisely for this reason that Deústua held that the Hellenic ideal constituted from the very start a unique compenetration in which liberty views order under the guise of harmony: " . . . order is explained by liberty itself in the particular form of harmony, of oneness and of multiplicity, coexisting without destroying each other and, on the contrary, fortifying each other because of that conciliation" (1, 23). This instilled desire for harmony reveals the reason behind the Greeks' instinctive abhorrence of movement and plurality.[4]

4. This ideal, Deústua affirmed, stemmed from the Greeks' refusal to let themselves be possessed by any one aspect of life and explains why they introduced reason in imagination, thought in feeling, reflection in passion. The Hellenic spirit, fired by a lively and inexhaustible curiosity and delicateness of soul, inspired the Greeks to think with sensibility and to imagine with clarity. The above factors left no room for extreme, excessive views either in philosophy or in imaginative works such as mythology and art (1, 27).

The idea of order and harmony formed their aesthetic ideal. It was incarnated in their works of art; they believed that it is generated by a life lived freely, without compulsion, within the limits prescribed by "methodical reason" ("razón ordenadora") (1, 23). Consequently, liberty as such can play only a secondary role. Its importance pales before the brightness of the well-ordered intelligence.

Deústua emphasized the aesthetic element in Greek thought. He speculated that the aesthetic ideal of harmony influenced all other aspects of Greek life. Not only was their ideal of the universe aesthetic but their moral conscience was also fused with a feeling for the beautiful. Greek rationality, unifying the multiplicity and heterogeneity of the external as well as the internal world, created harmony everywhere. The good, which the will perceived as a supreme end, became synonymous with harmony, and the latter constituted unity in diversity. The fusion of the two apparently exclusive activities, imagination and reflection, is explained by the Greek delight in clear perception. Deústua believed that Greek perception did not admit detail as detail but only as an integral part of a well-combined system. Greek art did not and could not escape the Greek intellect, and it must therefore be considered as eminently contemplative. The pleasure it produces springs from the equilibrium obtained through "the aesthetic synthesis of static liberty . . . " (1, 25). Deústua denied that static liberty is the equivalent of autodetermination. Rather, he viewed it as the lack of coercion, the negative form of liberty, that results from a "perfectly developed life" (1, 25). The Hellenic plastic imagination was satisfied with such an ideal. And this concept of liberty explained the ideal that the Greeks had not only of order but also of living harmony. For Deústua, then, the notion of static liberty was the essential trait of the Hellenic spirit.

Gradually, the aesthetic order just described was superseded by the philosophical, logical order. Mythology lost its poetic value and divine meaning; systematic mythology, guided by reason, replaced anthropomorphism. And reason, finding the existing pantheism unsatisfactory, aspired to monism. Thus Deústua contended that Greek philosophy did not result from an autonomous impulse; he suggested that Greek thought instead traversed the moral or practical order before embarking on pure abstraction. In fact, he saw the moral order as a transitional state between the aesthetic order and the logical order of science. This passage is marked by lyric and gnomic poetry "which comprised as a norm the philosophy of human life" (1, 32). To sustain the opposite—that is, that philosophical speculation arose simply from observing the physical world— would be, as he put it, to "forget the social element, which gave rise to political life with its ideal of liberty, of liberty which in philosophy is translated as the emancipation of the spirit from the mythical tradition" (1, 32).

In dealing with the intellectual movements in Greece, Deústua's overriding interest in the will and inner freedom led him to focus his attention on the Greek Golden Age of philosophy. Prior to this period, he admitted, the multiplicity of philosophical schools from Thales of Miletus to Parmenides of Elea created a movement of spiritual emancipation. He underscored, however, that they also created a crisis which temporarily paralyzed the Greek mind, in regard to the problem of knowledge. The advent of the Peloponnesian war, symbol for Deústua of the internal disintegration of the Greek spirit, heightened this crisis. The dissolution of the national character, in turn, gave support to the Sophists, who proposed a philosophy based on relativism. A distinction arose between nature (the eternally identical) and human convention, which was judged to have only a historical value. Skepticism quickly spread throughout Attica as civil and moral laws relinquished their claim to universality. In their stead, the Sophists substituted individual determination, driven by a natural impulse and not by free will, and proclaimed it the law of nature as well as the supreme law of human conduct. Notwithstanding the dire dissolutive consequences of this school, Deústua found a positive side to sophistry. He was convinced that the Sophists destroyed the mental support for polytheism, eliminated the ingenious dogmatism of fantastic speculation, obliged philosophers to define both the true object of thought and the method of conceiving it, and paved the road for the anthropological period of Socratic moral philosophy.

With Socrates, Greek thought returned to the universal validity of reason and truth over desire and passion. It did so, however, seeking to promote the cause of morality and not to extol the merits of pure reason. Identifying virtue with knowledge, Socrates equated happiness with the knowledge of the good. Thus Deústua now found man pursuing freedom, or the emancipation of the soul—but doing so at the expense of his will, since this intellectual conception of the will demands its submission to law and morality. Choice, or autodetermination of the will, as conceived by Socratic thought, played no part in the acquisition of virtue. Consequently, Deústua concluded that Socrates' intellectualism promotes determinism. His absolute faith in the power of reason to find goodness and happiness reduces liberty, which for Deústua is action, to the state of obligation.

If Socrates' role was that of physician to the Greek mind, curing it of skepticism, the role of his disciple Plato was that of a soldier battling the fortifications of the senses in order to enthrone the real world of Ideas. With Plato, philosophy reached a period of systematization in which the problem of knowledge was more perfectly solved and in which the principle of order was elevated to the category of the "universal principle of explication" (1, 70). Deústua saw Plato as tending toward the Eleatic School in his affirmation that only the perfect exists within which "*being* and *knowledge* are one and the same" (1, 71). Plato identified Ideas with the forms of the good and reduced the universe to a unified system based on an eternal reason, to a synthesis of relationships, without which the intelligible, immutable world would be replaced by chaos. In other words, what Plato tried to establish was the supreme synthesis of perfection, intelligibility, and reality. The objects of metaphysics present not only what is or could be but also what ought to be. Thus, according to Deústua, Plato introduced the concept of moral value as a supreme idea, presened it as order and not liberty. Since reason in its ascending dialectic process never reaches the stage of liberty, Plato's man ultimately is not free to choose either the general or particular end of his actions, once reason has shown him what these ends consist of. The will, therefore, cannot be free; it is necessarily consistent with knowledge or wisdom and is consequently only concerned with being and the good. The will, denied of any tendency other than that of the good dictated by reason is, therefore, not free. As for choice, or what one would now call free will, Deústua noted that Plato considered it an imperfection because it is prone to error.

Like Plato, Aristotle tried to solve the problems of intelligibility, but his solutions varied markedly from Plato's. Deústua observed that Aristotelian harmony is essentially aesthetic and that Aristotle saw the elements as realities, not as pure concepts. The most important and perfect being is not, for Aristotle, the empty form, but pure actuality, the activity which fulfills all of its potential. The logical norm is created by reason and is dependent on it. Aristotle reintroduced in the material world the forms which Plato had mistakenly substantialized. What Plato had objectified, Aristotle presented as a subjective phenomenon of the human intellect. Yet Deústua insisted that, just as in Plato's thought, order dominates the Aristotelian system because the same principle of "methodical reason" still determines the norm of human life. Although a virtuous action is dependent on man, and must be so to be a voluntary decision, this free activity receives its form from reason. It is through reason that the will conducts man from his imperfect state of potentiality toward the state of perfection or actuality; it is reason which determines the ethical object of preference for man. Liberty, before the imperative force of thought, simply does not exist.

Reason is free, and it alone can lead man to the knowledge of
the good, perfect, and divine. The will is consequently identified with reason that desires, a force that submits itself to the
"rational principle," to God—the Being of complete actuality
disengaged from all potentiality who produced universal-
aesthetic order. Seeking the life that best exemplifies the
perfect will, Aristotle chose the contemplative life of the
scholar. Above all others, it is the scholar who experiences
the liberty of pure actuality in his rational contemplation of
God's aesthetically ordered universe. Thus intellectual pleasure constitutes the essence of aesthetic feeling, and both are
unified, finally, in the moral order which for Deústua's Aristotle is the order of the beautiful. Virtue is excellence, perfection; at the same time, it is proportion, order, the mean
"between that which is excessive and deficient" (1, 123).

In Deústua's treatment of Greek philosophy, its aesthetic
conception is clearly what most powerfully attracted him to
the classical world. As a philosopher who would later proclaim
dynamic aesthetics as the pinnacle of all philosophical speculation, Deústua was a strong admirer of the magnificent
aesthetic structure with which the Greeks endowed the universe. The attraction, however, was not uncritical. The Greek
vision of static liberty, of proportion and harmony, stems from
the restraints imposed by reason and determinism upon free
will. The Hellenic soul waded into the stream of liberty;
Hellenic reason froze it. Consequently, the Greek mind,
Deústua reluctantly conceded, failed to extol the ideal of
liberty. Rather, it continued to see order as the most important principle of life.

From Deústua's point of view, then, one of the main
problems that antiquity left unresolved was how to bring free
will into harmony with the established order of providence.
The two main figures who took on the task to find a solution
to this problem were Saint Augustine and Saint Thomas
Aquinas. Both of them, Deústua noted, developed the issue
as a combat between dogma and free will. Saint Augustine's
stand was a dual one. As a representative of the Church,

he always kept its dogma in mind. But as a philosopher, he concentrated his efforts on the *"principle of certitude of consciousness"* (2, 20). Deústua recognized that Saint Augustine introduced for the first time the psychological principle of self-awareness as the starting point of philosophy. Under the influence of ethical-religious ideas, metaphysical interest turns from the world without to the world within and psychological questions replace metaphysical ones. The idea of the will and its role now become all important. Not only did Saint Augustine find the will in all states and movements of the soul, but he also equated the soul with the will itself. Freely created in God, man's will is a free cause. Liberty, then, depends on man himself, namely, on his will. This position, Deústua pointed out, logically forced Saint Augustine to expand unilaterally the dominant position of the will to cover the "entire representative and cognitive process" (2, 21). As a result, even rational thought, with its judgments and deductions, is ultimately dependent on the will's objectives. It is now the will and not rational knowledge that maps out the direction and goal of thought. Hence, Saint Augustine's antideterminist and antirationalist stand as a philosopher-psychologist was manifestly plain to Deústua.

Deústua, however, acknowledged that the sympathetic portrait he had drawn of Saint Augustine was incomplete. The soul of Saint Augustine was a battleground where liberty and order actively vied for hegemony. As a man, as a philosopher, psychologist, and moralist, Deústua considered Saint Augustine an ardent voluntarist, a fervent supporter of free will. But when Saint Augustine donned his theological frock and attempted to save his fellowman for God, these qualities quickly began to fade; under the cloak of religious redemption, he became the great defender of order and the inclement prosecutor of free will. Deústua found that, as a theologian, Saint Augustine reduced man to a composite of reason and passion; he was convinced that reason should dominate passion because reason by its very essence is superior to passion. When reason dominates, the soul ascends toward things intelligible, eternal, and immutable; when passion dominates, the soul desires that which is only sensible and fleeting. Given the fact that free will accounts for such desire, both passion and free will are necessarily a fault and not a sign of perfection in man. From a theological point of view, then, free will gives rise to disorder within the soul; it is a power within man that affects his moral state. Going one step further, Deústua claimed that Saint Augustine was in reality a fatalist. Man, in Saint Augustine's eyes, is not free. On the one hand he cannot escape from the orders of God or the dictates of reason; nor, on the other hand, can he flee from the allurements of the devil or the inclinations of passion. The Church Father conceded little to natural man: only resolution and intention. When resolution and intention are exercised for the good, man, working through God's grace, conforms to reason and is free. What man freely wants is to obtain beatitude, transcendent happiness in the possession of the eternal and immutable good. To seek that which is but a fleeting good—that is, when resolution and intention follow the dictates of passion / free will—is to lean toward egotism, toward desire, toward sin and thereby toward nonbeing. Thus, paradoxically, for Saint Augustine free will is only apparently free: without God's grace, he can will only evil. The human will does not acquire grace through liberty; rather, liberty is attained through grace.

For Deústua, whatever inroads Saint Augustine made in the domain of the internal world of consciousness, the Church soon swept away. The conflict between faith and reason ended with reason completely accepting the dictum of the Christian dogma and sacrificing inner liberty at the altars of the imperious Church. The all-powerful Church became an organized and fortified body whose pedagogical mission demanded absolute and total adherence to its unyielding authority. Seeking to propagate its ecclesiastical ideology through systematic thought, the Church turned to Scholastic philosophy for support and strength.

Among the Christian thinkers, Saint Thomas Aquinas, in Deústua's estimation, served the cause of the Church best: as a champion of order, he envisioned the universe as good because God has placed in it real and admirable order. According to Aquinas, rationality directs life's pattern of existence. The intellect, understanding the idea of the good and knowing in particular what it is, determines the will and constitutes the *supremus motor* of psychical life. As an ethical ideal, liberty is assumed to be a necessity, founded on knowledge. And freedom of choice is conceivable if the intelligence offers the will diverse means of obtaining a given end. The ordering of means, essentially an intellectual act, presupposes four things: knowledge of the end; knowledge of the means to reach it; the ability to discover the relationships between the two; and the adoption of the act best suited to obtain the determined end. Deústua concluded that for Saint Thomas Aquinas, reason and reflection reveal the true will, that they create liberty in man. God's role here is limited. Although He knows what man ought to do, God never forces his action or his decision: "Dios sabe lo que debemos hacer, pero sin hacer necesarias nuestras acciones, ni nuestra elección. El prevée todo lo que debe ser y cómo debe ser; es decir, las cosas necesarias, como necesarias, las posibles, como posibles y las acciones libres, como libres. Así no debe haber entre la presciencia divina y el libre albedrío ninguna especie de desacuerdo" (2, 52). In the divine plan, morality ought to exist, but it cannot exist without free will. The latter is thus indispensable to divine order and does not oppose Divine Providence. Deústua further observed that Aquinas even applied his intellectual determinism to God Himself: although God is eternal, omniscient, and omnipotent, still, in Him all is immutable and necessary. God's will is not synonymous with arbitrariness; it is identical to necessity, just as human will is. As a result, divine will is also subordinated to reason, and the world is the necessary product of its essence.

In short, Deústua inferred that for the Christian man liberty is essentially a moral postulate at the service of God.

The Church proclaimed man free in order to hold him responsible for his actions. Deústua argued that Christianity's greatest achievement lies in having engendered "that principle of interiority which made man conscious of his personal self" (2, 67). It elevated the individual and oriented him toward liberty. But this liberty only freed man from the external world; it did not stimulate the "truly creative activity of one's capabilities" (2, 67). In fact, during the Middle Ages, the Church absorbed and dominated man completely, subordinating all forms of existence—the physical, psychical, and political orders—to divine thought and order at the expense of inner freedom.

With the advent of the Renaissance, philosophy broke with the Scholastic notion of revelation, encouraged the principle of self-awareness, and developed a cult of individualism heretofore unknown. Nonetheless Deústua alleged that the Renaissance did not really affirm the integral liberty of the spirit. Intellectualism continued to dominate man's cultural activities and order still served as the axis around which the spirit's action revolved. Man either perceived the world from an artistic point of view or sought a scientific explanation of life based on the laws of nature. The aesthetic conception surfaced first in cosmology under the guidance of Nicholas of Cusa and later under the genius of Giordano Bruno. Both men envisioned the world as a work of art, as a work of mathematical perfection set up by God. The divine unity of universal life led to the admiration of the macrocosmos as a manifestation of divine ideas. As a result, the progress made in understanding nature through a mechanistic interpretation of phenomena failed to advance the cause of freedom. Stressing mathematical inferences and data of sense experience, the mechanistic outlook simply meant a greater intellectual understanding of what was still considered to be a divine creation. The emphasis thus placed on reason not only gave it hegemony over the other human faculties, but also eventually made these dependent on the intellect itself. Finally, the aesthetic notion of nature fell prey to the scientific (rational) or logical conception of the world, wherein order predominated, subordinating or eliminating totally the ideal of freedom. This tendency continued with Francis Bacon, Thomas Hobbes, and more emphatically with René Descartes.

From Deústua's point of view Descartes only apparently made use of liberty as the starting point of his philosophical system. Deústua contended that Descartes used the term liberty in a dual sense which, ironically, ends by negating its very existence: ". . . en el primero, significa el poder de decidirse entre dos contradictorios: hacer o no hacer, afirmar o negar . . . ; en el segundo, quiere decir el poder de conformarse a su verdadera naturaleza de hacer lo mejor, de afirmar lo verdadero, de huir del mal" (2, 73–74). Deústua argued that this amounts to negating the power of choice between two contraries and reduces freedom merely to an inclination toward one of them, be it because one knows that the good and the true lie with one side, or because "God so disposes the interiority of thought" (2, 73). Yet for Descartes it would seem that divine grace and natural knowledge do not diminish liberty; they fortify it. The indifference or spiritual indetermination that one feels when not drawn to either one or another side marks, for Descartes, the lowest degree of liberty and must be considered the result of insufficient knowledge rather than a sign of the will's perfection. Like Socrates, Descartes maintained that knowledge of the good or the true eliminates deliberation and choice. Since the will can only naturally desire the good, it will embrace the good and the true even more freely when it perceives them clearly. The will, placed face to face with the good, can never remain indifferent. For indifference arises, as has been stated, from ignorance. As the good is preestablished by God, man's intelligence, for Descartes, would have only one task to perform: to "present to us this good toward which our will naturally turns" (2, 74).

To underscore his conception of rational determinism—a

philosophical position defended even more intensely later by Baruch Spinoza and Gottfried Wilhelm Leibniz—Descartes fell back on theology. God, Descartes declared, is the author of all actions, including those dependent on human will. If it were not so, if something could in fact occur in the world that did not emanate from God, then God would be imperfect. Obviously this puts free will at odds with divine omniscience and omnipotence. Descartes' attempt to reconcile the two, Deústua noted, was in line with familiar Scholastic thinking of his time. He posited the existence of two wills. The first, from which the occurrence of all things arises, is absolute and independent and pertains exclusively to God. The second will, found in man, is relative in nature and determines his merit or demerit.

As for liberty, Deústua affirmed that Descartes' metaphysical ideas simply exclude it. According to his theory of continuous creation, at every instant God is creating the world of bodies and of souls. Nothing is done or, for that matter, can be done without Him. And because the continuous creation is immutable, it makes liberty impossible. Essentially, then, the dominating idea in the Cartesian system, Deústua concluded, is that of a logical, mathematical order founded on divine will. Consequently, the universe is based on inflexible laws (a mechanistic outlook) and the most that man can aspire to is to change his desires, never the order of the world. Supreme happiness would lie in conforming one's actions to divine will, in fusing human will and intelligence with those of God. Herein for Descartes resides man's freedom. However, as Deústua emphasized, this concept of emancipation must not be mistaken for liberty. For Descartes' God, through His will and intelligence, orders the universe according to unchangeable laws, and this eliminates any principle of indetermination. Within Descartes' formulation, only God would be free. He alone would have absolute liberty and absolute power of creativity, producing the existence, as well as the essence and laws, of things.

Nevertheless, Deústua granted that an important change took place with Descartes. Necessity is no longer considered an absolute. It has been replaced by freedom, thought of now as absolute and primordial. This freedom, however, is not attributed to man but only, as stated above, to God: "Es a Dios que atribuye la libertad primitiva, de donde sale todo lo demás. La necesidad que percibimos en los axiomas de lógica y de metafísica proviene de nosotros que encontramos la verdad toda hecha, la esencia como una ley impuesta a nuestra inteligencia, en lugar de sentirnos como el origen de la verdad y de sus leyes. Si Dios ha querido que algunas verdades fuesen necesarias lo ha querido libremente" (2, 78).

While philosophy on the Continent was largely rationalistic, in England it was adopting an empiricist and materialist approach. This, too, as Deústua indicated, locked out the notion of liberty. Francis Bacon, the father of inductivism, could not profess liberty if he was to be consistent in his approach, for liberty did not enter as a factor in the natural sciences. Induction as a method sought to discover the laws governing nature through observation of experiential facts and observable phenomena. This blind faith in the science of the concrete drove Thomas Hobbes to reduce all phenomena, including spiritual ones, to movement, to physicomathematical terms. Since his mechanistic theory considered only that which was corporeal to be real, Hobbes dismissed psychical occurrences as simple products of fantasy—as mere appearances of phantasms—and proclaimed (erroneously, as far as Deústua was concerned) that only sensation constituted the source of knowledge and the point of departure for science. Hobbes's materialistic outlook logically excluded the ideal that liberty was an inherent quality of the human soul. Deústua claimed that this was substantiated by Hobbes's psychological analysis of the will and by his investigation of the reality of the free will, which he identified with the strongest impelling desire.

The empiricist John Locke, in turn, focused his attention

on the theory of knowledge and on empirical psychology, since he deemed that an inquiry into the possibilities of human knowledge constituted the necessary prerequisite to all metaphysical speculations. This radical turn to subjectivity provided a unique opportunity to reexamine the problem of liberty. But, as Deústua observed, the promising chance lamentably came and went without resolving the problem of liberty. Locke's distinction between the will and freedom (both for him are active but different powers derived from internal experience) converted the will into the active power of the soul over the body and relegated freedom to acting or not acting conformably to a choice or a judgment of the spirit. In the final analysis, Deústua argued that Locke asserted not only that liberty supposes reason and will but also that reason, discerning between good and evil desires, has the power of dictating imperative motives to the will. Under these circumstances, freedom would consist solely in the emancipation from alien moral coercion and not from the rigid, logical norms of thought. Such a view of liberty was, understandably, unacceptable to Deústua.

Another strong blow against the idea of liberty was struck by David Hume, who led radical empiricism to its final consequences through the methodology of the clear idea. Evidently inspired by Locke, Hume defined liberty as the power to act under the impulse of certain motives or passions (which at best may be guided by, but which never arise from, reason) when no impediment hinders this action. As for the notion that man is conscious of liberty, that liberty actually exists, this in Hume's mind is nothing more than an illusion, a false impression fostered by reflection. According to Deústua, Hume's pitiless criticism of science and metaphysics leaves man only with instinct and nature as a practical guide. At best, then, the foundation of morality, for Hume, lies in a natural instinct which would determine, under the guise of taste or sentiment, the good or the bad in terms of general (not personal or egotistical) utility.

While the concept of order prevailed in the eighteenth century, two figures, Jean-Jacques Rousseau and Immanuel Kant (the first minor, the second major) apparently—but only apparently—emphasized the concept of liberty. Deústua's reaction toward Rousseau was strikingly ambivalent. On the one hand, he could not help but sympathize with his anti-intellectual stand. On the other hand, the lack of philosophic rigor in Rousseau's reasoning and his pragmatic and immanentist tendencies disturbed Deústua. As a champion of liberty, Rousseau opposed the dominating forces of reason —materialism and fatalism; he based his system ostensibly on liberty, giving priority to feeling and will. Through feeling (sentiment), man, for Rousseau, immediately perceives the existence of God, liberty, and immortality. Rousseau's basic tenet—that the principle of action resides in the will of a free being—makes the concept of necessity meaningless. This anti-intellectual position naturally appealed to Deústua, who was a voluntarist and a devotee of Bergsonian irrationalism. Nevertheless, Deústua rejected Rousseau even as he admitted that Rousseau exalted liberty in his social and political works. The problem lay not so much in the apparent contradiction between the individual and general will (man never loses his absolute autonomy, according to Rousseau, even though he must perforce surrender his will in favor of the general will) but rather in the fact that Rousseau ultimately placed the will under the supervision of reason in order to legitimize all sentimental needs. For Deústua then, Rousseau negated (unwittingly, to be sure), indeterminism in favor of rational determinism.

By the time Kant appeared on the philosophical scene, philosophy had undergone profound changes. According to Deústua, the universal character of philosophy, as it appeared in antiquity and to some degree was retained in the works of Bacon and Descartes, had disappeared. Philosophic inquiry pushed aside metaphysical problems and turned its attention to logical ones; while scientific knowledge, in both its empirical and its mathematical aspect, reigned supreme. Faced with this transformation in philosophy, Kant set out to harmonize the two opposing epistemological views represented by rationalists on the one hand and by empiricists on the other. From Kant's point of view, both were dogmatic in their theory of knowledge. Both believed that nature could be known in an absolute manner: according to rationalism, solely through reason; according to empiricism, solely through sensations. His own philosophic speculations, however, refuted that reason alone provided man with absolute knowledge and that sensation alone proved knowledge to be a synthetic activity of reason acting on the data of intuitions. He insisted that knowledge had to be a composite of both experience and a priori forms of thought.

Unfortunately, Kant's solution to the problems he faced did not, Deústua stated, further the purposes of freedom. Following in the footsteps of the rationalists, he placed reason above the other spiritual faculties, such as the will, making it impossible for Deústua to consider him a champion of liberty. Deústua argued that within Kant's philosophical system, moral laws, however they differ from physical laws, are to the realm of the will what pure laws of understanding are to the realm of intelligence. Both are universal and necessary. What Kant did, then, was to explain the value of morality without appealing to its object; he looked not for the matter (purpose) but for the form of law (pure obligation). Such a position was unacceptable to Deústua, as it supposed the will to be free only to the extent that it allows itself to be determined by the form of a law. Neither did Deústua admit Kant's logical conclusion that when the above takes place, liberty and moral law are one. If they were, liberty would be a transcendental principle and would be conceivable only in noumenal terms. This in turn would imply that nothing could be known about it, that no explanation could be given to show how it would be possible, that its reality could never be proven. Consequently, Deústua argued that although Kant placed great importance on practical reason (will), although he considered liberty important, liberty was not the primary object of his philosophical system. He was not, as it were, a psychologist seeking to understand the nature of thought, will, and feeling, but rather a logician attempting to discover within reason itself the foundation of all logic, of all morality, and of all aesthetics. In short, Deústua saw Kant's work as the last and most profound attempt to solve philosophy's most arduous problem, namely, that of viewing "necessity in reality as a rational necessity . . ." (2, 157). The latter, of course, would explain why Kant, in the last resort, denied that liberty is a fact of experience and why he subordinated his theory of liberty to his theory of a priori knowledge.

After Kant, Germany wallowed in the doldrums of reason and order during the first half of the nineteenth century. Sounding a dissonant chord, Arthur Schopenhauer expounded an irrationalist view and became the exception to that rule. Interestingly enough, Schopenhauer, who replaced Hegel's Idea with Will as the principle of everything, left no mark on Deústua. Deústua maintained that Schopenhauer tore himself away from rational determinism only to fall prey to yet another form of determinism—that of a blind, universal, and eternal power of life and growth. Moreover, Schopenhauer raised the voice of pessimism and nihilism. He called on man, helplessly trapped in the painful web of suffering, to destroy the will to live by escaping from life, by denying consciousness, especially through Buddhistic contemplation. In sharp contrast, Deústua—foremost a philosopher of vitality and beauty, which he identified as the most perfect expression of psychological freedom—was incapable of denying the energy of life, of considering any view that willfully sought to promote anguish in man. This fact, perhaps, may explain why Deústua omitted from his analysis such preexistential philosophers as Frederick Nietzsche and Sören Kierkegaard.

If, in Germany, Schopenhauer was out of step with his

time, G. W. F. Hegel certainly set its tempo. Although he was to leave an indelible imprint on Deústua's aesthetic ideas, in all other respects Deústua was unreceptive to Hegel's idealistic pantheism, which carried Kantian transcendental idealism to its extreme logical conclusion. Nothing could have been more foreign to Deústua's voluntarist Weltanschauung than the assertions made by Hegel that "whatever is rational is real," "All reality is rational." For in Hegel's identification of thought and being, which are also Idea and Spirit, Deústua found himself enveloped in a rational deterministic world, a world where Spirit, through a dialectical movement of thesis, antithesis, and synthesis, manifests itself in the concrete universe. In this world, Deústua stressed, the individual enjoys, at best, a relative, limited freedom. He is but a mere particle of Spirit, which only in its final stage of evolution can acquire full liberty. Following in Kant's footsteps, Hegel continued to conceive of freedom in purely a priori terms. Epitomizing the most extreme form of rationalism, Hegel had little use for psychology as a science of the self and its faculties. Deústua's closing remark—"Hegelian philosophy, then, does not deal with psychological freedom" (2, 199)—comes, therefore, as no surprise.

While Germany embraced Hegel's extreme rationalism, the rest of Europe followed in the footsteps of Francis Bacon and English empiricism, taking up Kant's dictum that only science renders knowledge of the external physical world possible. For Deústua it was a period steeped in the murky waters of positivism. As a philosophical movement positivism did not bother to grapple with the problem of inner liberty, namely, with the notion of indeterminism. Indeed, the positivists, sticking fast to the raw data of experience, abrogated liberty—dismissing the concept of liberty as a mere illusion of the mind—and replaced it with the doctrine of strict determinism. Logical thought prevailed, imposing a rigorous order on all facets of experience, and necessity became the guiding light of all ethical, aesthetic, and scientific investigation. The "how" replaced the "why," and thinkers began to frown upon the mere idea that the imagination had the power to create capricious worlds at will. This new thrust, which finally placed science—if only temporarily—on the highest pedestal of human knowledge, arose mainly from two centers, France and England.

Seeking to synthesize the ensemble of sciences, Auguste Comte became the unrivaled spokesman for this movement in France. Perfunctorily reviewing Comte's social philosophy, Deústua spurned it completely. His strong personal dislike of Comte stemmed from the nefarious influence which Comte's philosophy had had, and still continued to have, on his homeland, and showed plainly when he referred to Comte as "the enemy of liberty" (2, 211). A devotee of artistic creativity, Deústua flatly rejected Comte's psychological stand denying consciousness unlimited freedom. He also discarded Comte's extravagant assertion that positivism would restore the spiritual and social harmony undermined in Europe by modern criticism and the French revolution and, furthermore, would put an end to the social anarchy of his time. For all Comte's glorification of humanity, Deústua nevertheless pictured the creator of modern sociology as the philosopher for whom ethical laws preside over social order and for whom the universal arrangement of things forcefully dictates the rules of individual conduct.

In England, those principally responsible for firmly implanting the idea of determinism were John Stuart Mill and Herbert Spencer. Deústua alleged that Mill, while allowing the will to modify man's actions, in reality never considered it a causal agent. For Mill the will is totally dependent on the force of desire; that is, it is determined by external factors. Consequently Mill envisioned man as an intermediary agent of his character at best, never as a free agent. Every act can be traced to a motive (a desire) that triumphs over another and the will thus is transformed into nothing more than a movement produced by a dominant sensation. Free will, as the essential constituent of consciousness, becomes an empty, useless concept, a patent absurdity in Mill's philosophical system, thus making psychological or moral freedom an equally absurd postulate. Deústua concluded that to accept the philosophical view of Mill would amount to accepting mental determinism or necessity.

Although Mill's position was extreme, Deústua felt that Spencer established an even more radical outlook, as he introduced the mechanical principle of universal evolution to explain reality where cause and effect have a direct and real relationship. The basic axiom of Spencer's theory is that the same quantity of energy is conserved at all times in the universe. Deústua maintained this would lead him to conclude that present moments or phenomena are the exact equation of past ones and that future phenomena or movements will be nothing more than the consequence of the rigorous equation of the present. Thus, movements arising from man's will—in fact, the will itself—depend completely on past movements. As a result, man cannot create any movement, nor, for that matter, can he modify the direction of any movement. Therefore, free will does not, and cannot, exist. External media alone determine the inner self; order reigns within every class of phenomena; and man, thus degraded, is transformed into an automaton, a creature whose actions are always mechanically fixed.

Barely had this scientific conception of the universe taken root when, at the close of the nineteenth century, a violent reaction against it took place among European thinkers. They were unwilling to leave man chained to an inexorable, blind, unswerving force, and a new wave of philosophic doctrines emerged to recover for the individual his supposed lost freedom. For Deústua this movement reached its zenith in psychology with Wilhelm Wundt and in philosophy with Henri Bergson. Both men made a lasting imprint on Deústua, whose *Estética general* sprang from the assimilation of their ideas.

It was the psychologist, not the philosopher Wundt who

fascinated Deústua. What drew him to Wundt, the founder of voluntarist psychology, was that Wundt studied the totality of experience in its immediate character and accented the role that volition plays in the psychic process. Deústua accepted Wundt's assertion that the whole of psychic life consists of a continuous series of new creations wherein the will is an autonomous fact originating from immediate experience. This stance led Wundt to conceive of the will not as a function that is added on to representation, feelings, impulses, and desires, but rather as something contained in them already. Essentially, both thinkers acknowledged no difference between impulses and desires on the one hand and will on the other. The volitional act is thereby identified with apperception. Admitting that consciousness cannot exist without apperception, Wundt, and Deústua with him, immediately inverted the statement and concluded that consciousness is equally unfeasible without volitional activity. If Deústua accompanied Wundt the pscyhologist up to here, he parted company with Wundt the philosopher when Wundt theorized that the collective will binds and determines individual evolution. Thus, in the last analysis, Deústua declared that Wundt had failed to shed the last remnants of positivism and had concluded by subordinating liberty to an outside order.

As important as Wundt was to his psychological formation, ideologically Deústua was most indebted to Henri Bergson. One of the first supporters of Bergson in South America, Deústua applauded his absolute agnosticism of the intellect and his contention that the problem of liberty must be presented and solved within the realm of psychology. Herein lay the magnetic attraction that Bergson had for Deústua. From a psychological point of view, Bergson affirmed that an analysis of "duration"—synonymous with continuity, inner time, heterogeneity—leads to the idea of liberty. Sympathetic to voluntarist psychology, Deústua heartedly agreed. Pure duration involves the succession of conscious states, where the self lets itself live and refuses to split the present from the past.

Having denied succession to external phenomena, Bergson—and by identification Deústua—insisted that the multiplicity of external phenomena exist only insofar as consciousness is capable of retaining them as a whole (that is, in a state of duration), or as displacements in space (that is, homogeneous time).

Opposing the deterministic-mechanistic point of view which presupposed distinct and successive parts in consciousness as well as a regulating cause-effect relationship between thoughts and sentiments, Bergson and Deústua exalted the idea of dynamism, regarding liberty as a real activity. Thus an act achieves the highest degree of liberty when, unfettered by reason, it stems from the fundamental self and thereby encompasses the whole of man's personality. The apperception of liberty, then, is immediate (intuitive), but is lost when reason intervenes. Indeed, when reason is present the flow of life or duration becomes fixed and reality offers only a depthless frozen section for the intellectual microscope to analyze. The relationship between the profound self and the act is undefinable precisely because the process of change is what makes man free. Liberty is an absolute or causal principle. Following Bergson, Deústua proclaimed that liberty "is a fact and among the verifiable facts the most evident of them all" (2, 254). Consequently, in Deústua's philosophic terminology, liberty, duration, personality, consciousness, and will are synonymous terms.

Free, man is like a surfer. He rides the present wave, whose advancing crest swells with his past, rolling him toward undetermined future shores. Man is naught without his vital past, without his pure memory. (Rote memory or habit gives birth exclusively to the superficial self because it unconsciously repeats, in a mechancial fashion, past patterns in a present.) Pure memory brings forth the past, spontaneously recalled from its virtual state, to infuse, expand, and enrich the present durational flow of the self. Pure memory—Deústua preferred to call it "creative imagination" (2, 255)—

endures and thereby constitutes the fundamental and free self in a creative present.

Deústua enthusiastically traveled this far with Bergson but no further. Bergson proceeded immediately to deny that memory is a function of the brain. This metaphysical supposition eventually led him to the mystical hypostatization that the universe is one great consciousness in a state of perpetual change and to the assertion that Real Duration, or the eternally dynamic, is synonymous with Being, the creator of all reality and life. Deústua, on the other hand, was more reserved, content to remain purely within the limits of the human camp. Exalting memory's imaginative power, the creative impulse which reveals the true and profound personality of the self during its richest moments of existence, Deústua sought only to defend what is preeminent in man, namely, his human spirituality.

From the foregoing remarks, it is evident that, for Deústua, reason would be an inadequate initial tool to capture both the flux of human duration and man's communion with external reality. Left on its own, reason congeals movement and easily renders reality—internal as well as external—antiseptic, devoid of all vital impact. The great insights into life, those that reveal a mind of great sensibility and aptitude in discovering and understanding the human condition even in the most modest and humble of objects, must first stream forth from intuition or disinterested instinct. "Intuition," Deústua stated, paraphrasing Bergson, "guides us to the very interiority of life . . . " (2, 259). By relating objects spatially, reason by itself barely skims the surface of existence. To auscultate, to tap existence at its fullest, ripest moment, one must explore within. Man immerses himself in the current of creation, diving for a unique pearl to embody the expression of his unique experience. As in the case of life's secrets, to fathom a certain particle of time's reality (in a time that is itself irreversible) is a deed that pertains to intuition alone.

To the question "Who perceives reality as a state of

continuous creation?" Deústua unequivocally replied, "The aesthetic soul." Only those enjoying artistic perception can insert themselves into their interiority with the necessary tension and intensity required to spiritualize matter. (It is evident, therefore, that Deústua differed from Bergson in this respect. Bergson maintained that that which is without possesses an interior essence and an eternal, independent, vital truth—a truth and essence not created but attentively grasped by the artist.) Through the artist, then, the object acquires new significance and depth. Having first gone beyond colors, sounds, and words to capture intuitively the inner essence of his vision, to view an object for what it has to offer in its human dimension, the artist then attempts, by every means available to him, to recreate objectively his vivid inner experience for his fellowman. Art, in this sense, can be reduced neither to matter (photographic replicas of external items) nor to the mechanics of composition (art for art's sake). Art leaps forward and attempts to snatch "movement in what is motionless, and life in death" (2, 269). Liberty becomes the aesthetic soul. The artist's soul is the bell that sounds forevermore. And so, leaving Bergson behind, Deústua energetically strode ahead and proclaimed that philosophy, whose object is liberty or duration, must first pass through the portals of art if it wishes to decipher the secrets of life.

# 4. The Aesthetic Conception

The books from which I learned to tell a story
do not communicate with each other—they are
like monads, Leibniz (another mathematician
and poet) would say—but they communicate
within me, reader and writer, origin of the
pre-established harmony in my private library.
My miniature stories are also monads, psychic
atoms in which is reflected, from different
perspectives, the totality of a view of life. Were
it coded, the key word would be: liberty.

Enrique Anderson Imbert
*Cage with Only One Side*

After the publication of *Las ideas de orden y de libertad*,
Deústua turned his attention completely to aesthetics, the
branch of human endeavor to which he had accorded primacy
among all other values. In 1923, at the age of seventy-four, an
age when most men have long since laid down their pen and
retired from intellectual life, Deústua published *Estética general*,
his most valuable contribution to the philosophic regeneration
of Peru. The work is divided into two parts. The first
part, "Sociología estética," can be subdivided, in turn, into
two sections: one, devoid of critical interest to our study, is
strictly expository and, by detailing objectively the aesthetic

59

ideas of such philosophers as Brunschwigg, Guyau, Fechner, Fouillée, Lalo, Basch, and Croce, merely serves as a general introduction to contemporary aesthetic theories; the other, subject to our analysis here, attempts to reveal the origin and psychic nature of what Deústua termed an aesthetic experience. The second part, "Cuestiones estéticas," sets forth and justifies beauty as the foremost human value and proclaims liberty as the first principle of aesthetics and philosophy.

## THE PSYCHOLOGICAL OUTLOOK

Deústua's psychological departure was of extreme importance. Within his Weltanschauung, emotional consciousness was not accessory but absolutely essential to life. Were it not, instinct alone would have sufficed to preserve the race of man by providing all the necessary tools needed for his subsistence. Or man might have been satisfied with recording reality in an intellectual mold, reality rendered under the umbrella of judgments of fact or of relation. In either instance, value judgments, which are dependent on appreciation, are absent. But Deústua's man lives not on bread alone. His life is centered around values, and without the world of emotional consciousness the possibility of worth and excellence vanishes altogether. Since beauty is a species of value for Deústua, it is inconceivable without emotional consciousness. To define beauty in other than empty terms, Deústua is convinced that one must offer answers to such questions as why, when, and how the beautiful manifests itself, what are the necessary conditions an object must fulfill before it can be considered beautiful, and what elements of man's nature make him sensitive to beauty. In short, Deústua believes that any philosophy of the beautiful, if it is to be a valid theory of values, must necessarily rest on firm psychological grounds. Herein, then, lies Deústua's deep interest in psychology and the reason behind his detailed analysis in Part 1 of the origin, place, and elements of the beautiful as an object of human experience.

*The Aesthetic Senses and
the Classification of Aesthetic Feelings*

Deústua's psychological basis of aesthetic activity demanded
that he establish a table of aesthetic sensations, differentiating
them from nonaesthetic ones. Consequently, his investigation
opened with a basic discussion of the senses. The questions he
had to answer at the outset of his inquiry were multiple and
the answers he provided affected his subsequent aesthetic
deliberations. For example, do man's senses provide a source
for aesthetic appreciation? If they do, to what extent are all
senses equal in their ability to capture and mentally translate
aesthetic qualities derived either from external reality or from
the internal world of the mind? What is the nature of the
qualities produced by the senses? Why are some sensations
aesthetic and others not? What is the relation between aesthetic senses and Deústua's basic tenet that liberty lies at the
heart of any aesthetic experience?

In Deústua's mind there was no doubt that there exist
aesthetic and nonaesthetic senses. The senses of taste, smell,
and touch are nonaesthetic because the sensations derived
from these three sources, like those stemming from visceral
organs and the muscular system, remain essentially unde-
fined, imprecise, and confusing. Fundamentally related to
vegetative functions, they rarely become conscious because
memory cannot readily isolate them and allow the intelligence
to discover their relationships.[1] The sensations from the

---

1. *Estética general* (Lima: Imprenta E. Rávago, 1923); all parentheti-
cal citations in the text of this chapter refer to this edition. Deústua,
however, recognized that there are times when the sensations from the
nonaesthetic senses appear to acquire an aesthetic property. Of the three
senses (taste, smell, and touch), taste (reduced to the sensual pleasure
arising from the act of nutrition) has little or no aesthetic import: "El papel
del gusto sería completamente nulo en estética, si algunas veces no desper-
tase en nosotros recuerdos, impresiones, completamente independientes
del efecto sensual, agradable o desagradable que provoca . . . " (pp. 170–
71). The olfactory sense is superior to taste: "Su papel estético es . . . un
poco más importante que el del gusto. El olfato, más que el gusto,

nonaesthetic senses are intimately tied to the actual biological state of the organ and to the external or internal irritant that triggers the feeling. At best, the sensations derived from the nonaesthetic senses reveal a simple state of either comfort and well-being or discomfort, without offering any precise idea of their objective causes. In the aesthetic senses, sight and hearing, the purely physical and subjective impression described above is nonexistent, the sensation being immediately transformed into a mental and objective image. Under normal circumstances these feelings "can promote the emotion of the beautiful" (p. 174). Sight and hearing offer to consciousness isolated (that is, individual), independent representations, perceived freely and then freely associated by the imagination. These representations, therefore, "are not only the most capable of making one feel that which is free in the expressions of objective reality, especially in that of the artistic [reality], but also [the most capable] of expressing, in a free and thereby beautiful form, the expansion of our psychic life" (p. 178).

The feelings derived from the representations, in turn, can be classified under two categories, elementary and superior aesthetic feelings. An advocate of the Wundtian experimental school of psychology, Deústua linked the elementary aesthetic feelings to isolated representations resulting from different combinations of sensations. Corresponding to the senses of hearing and sight, they rest essentially on the relationship of temporal and spatial representations. In the case of hearing, the elementary aesthetic feeling relates to harmony and rhythm. Deústua believed that only harmony

---

tiene la propiedad de evocar recuerdos: Un perfume nos recuerda antiguas impresiones, haciendo surgir un cuadro del pasado" (p. 171). Touch, in turn, is the sense most closely associated with aesthetic properties. For, through touch, even the blind can appreciate the aesthetic qualities of symmetry, repetition, and continuity in a piece of sculpture or in a decorative object of art. In short, the first two are only aesthetic insofar as they are able to stimulate memory to an aesthetic-pleasurable experience, whereas with touch, one can directly perceive simple aesthetic qualities.

produces psychological and thereby aesthetic satisfaction. Willfully ignoring the atonal revolution in music led by such figures as Schönberg and Stravinsky in the early twentieth century, Deústua insisted that prolonged dissonance and dis- harmony inevitably depress consciousness into a state of pain or displeasure. The same principle can be applied to rhythm: on the one hand, the repetition of related auditory represen- tations, after regular intervals of time, gives rise to pleasant states of consciousness. On the other hand, identical impres- sions produce a fatiguing effect which can never be identified with rhythm if repeated in pauses of equal duration; this also occurs when a series of heterogeneous impressions lack a unifying principle and make it difficult for the listener to grasp the unity of the piece with relative ease.[2]

Turning to visual representations, Deústua found that the aesthetic feeling does not depend on color or brightness alone, although these are important in producing the overall complex effect of an aesthetic experience. The elementary aesthetic feelings related to sight correspond to the disposi- tion or arrangement of forms and to the direction of contour lines.[3] Again relying on experimental psychology, Deústua

2. Contemporary physiology as well as psychology support Deústua's position: "Es un carácter inherente a nuestra naturaleza fisiológica, dice Soret, que toda sensación que se prolonga o que se repite indefinidamente deja de ser percibida por nosotros o llega a ser dolorosa. La variedad es absolutamente necesaria para reanimar nuestras impresiones y para impedir el efecto de embotamiento, muchas veces de dolor, que produce la mono- tonía de nuestras sensaciones, que sea en el orden físico o en el intelectual. En la percepción de lo bello, la *variedad* es, pues, una condición necesaria de placer, aunque condición negativa, según Soret, puesto que . . . la satisfacción placentera de lo bello nace de un principio de igualdad o de unidad, lo cual sucede en la armonía, en el ritmo, la simetría y la propor- ción, formas elementales de sentimientos estéticos, según el filósofo Wundt" (pp. 184–85).
3. This statement is difficult to reconcile with the following one, in which form and line are seen from the outset to play a minor role: "La luz y el color desempeñan un papel importantísimo en la representación estética de lo inorgánico. Los cristales hermosos, lo son, no tanto por sus for- mas regulares, sino por la apariencia de vida que les imprime la luz

asserted that with respect to simple forms, the eye prefers
regularity over irregularity. Symmetry, the simplest example
of regularity, is therefore present in every form that purports
to create an aesthetic effect. Deústua advocated a cause-effect
relationship, or at least the possibility that such a relationship
may be conditioned by environment, when he affirmed that
horizontal symmetry appeals most to man because he is accus-
tomed to observing in nature forms where this type of symmetry predominates. Thus horizontal symmetry will necessarily elicit greater aesthetic pleasure than vertically balanced
forms. In both instances, however, the effect is derived from
the repetition of homologous parts. As in music, Deústua
readily admitted, monotony can result from an overexaggera-
tion of symmetrical composition, or from a product which
depicts "incommensurable relationships."

Deústua also offered biological and psychological ex-
planations as to why unity and variety beget aesthetic pleasure. Biologically, he linked aesthetic pleasure with the life
process itself. Variety in unity and unity in variety are externally pleasing manifestations because they reflect two organic necessities, movement and rest: "Buscamos el reposo
por el movimiento; el ideal de felicidad ha consistido, pri-
mitivamente, en la tranquila satisfacción de las necesieades
biológicas, en la posesión tranquila de los medios para satis-
facerlas. La conservación, sin gasto, de las fuerzas adquiri-
das, produce el goce de bienestar; el movimiento, por sí
solo, no es agradable, sino cuando es fácil, cuando es un
juego y no un trabajo o cuando la espectativa de los frutos
del trabajo halaga la imaginación" (p. 345). Psychologically,
the relationship is based on the structural formation of the
psyche. For Deústua, man's psyche naturally organizes
things systematically: "nuestra naturaleza es una sistemati-
zación sistematizante" (p. 345). Awareness of the unity of

---

que reflejan y el color que los anima. Sugieren a la fantasía el movimiento
libre con esos elementos" (p. 494).

the self automatically gives rise to a pleasant feeling. This feeling increases when the soul is enriched by "harmonies or new systems of sensations" (p. 345) that have their origin in the external world.

While the relationships of temporal and spatial representations explain the intensity of aesthetic pleasure, Deústua asserted, they cannot explain the quantitative diversity of the aesthetic feeling. The latter receives its specific character from the particular content of the representations. Harmony, rhythm, and symmetry are pleasing because "the laws of multiplicity that these comprise awaken in man's spirit representations of aesthetic objects" (p. 182). These abstract relationships of forms are aesthetic objects of an undetermined content—but not because they are undetermined do they lack content. Deústua argued that, precisely for this reason, the abstract relationships of forms can participate vitally in the formation of complex aesthetic effects. In order that the aesthetic experience be as full as possible, form ought to correspond to content. Consequently, unity, variety, proportion (the compositional harmony of artistic elements in a work of art), although fundamental, are insufficient "to bring aesthetic consciousness to complete fruition" (p. 347). The artist must be capable of grasping by an act of disinterested intelligence the inner core of his object. The imagination then elevates the corresponding expressive formulation to an ideal order, or perfection. Form without content would render, at best, an "aesthetic sense of the pleasurable or an elementary aesthetic feeling . . . " (p. 348).

By the same token, Deústua was well aware that content must be organized to be meaningful. Hence, the abstract relationships described above do not constitute merely external principles of form. They are also ultimately responsible for bringing together the different parts of aesthetic content. The superior aesthetic feeling occurs when the work of art interfuses the elementary aesthetic feeling with logical, moral, and religious feelings. Envisioned in this manner, the superior aesthetic feelings encompass all other activities of the soul:

"Una obra de arte acabada pone en estado de tensión nuestro
sentimiento lógico, excita los sentimientos éticos y religiosos,
engendra emociones y sentimientos sensoriales y agrega todavía a esa combinación, en calidad de elementos con-
stitutivos esenciales, los sentimientos estéticos elementales,
que provienen del encadenamiento de representaciones su-
cesivas o de partes de una representación simultánea" (p.
185). Still, Deústua hastened to emphasize that this will produce superior aesthetic feelings only if the work fuses all the
elements into a harmonious and well-proportioned whole (a
view which he did not, however, hold consistently).[4] Since
the above cannot occur without the elementary aesthetic feelings, Deústua concluded that these feelings constitute the
nucleus of every aesthetic experience:

> Esta correlación en la que deben encontrarse las diversas
> formas de sentimiento, a fin de engendrar un sentimien-
> to estético total distinto es, al mismo tiempo, la causa de
> que sólo el sentimiento estético elemental sea apto para
> llegar a ser el factor de un efecto estético superior:
> porque las diversas *formas* de sentimiento estético ele-
> mental, a diferencia de las diversas formas de sen-
> timiento, tienen *afinidad* con las emociones como con
> los diversos sentimientos intelectuales, sea lógicos, moral-
> es o religiosos, sin que estén . . . comprendidas en
> esas formas las relaciones especiales con ciertas rep-

4. Indeed, Deústua later denied that the feeling of perfection is
necessarily related to that of the aesthetic. A work of art may be technically
perfect, yet the resultant feeling it inspires is not thereby inherently or
necessarily aesthetic: "Lo perfecto . . . no explica lo bello, ni se confunde
con él. El sentimiento de lo perfecto no es necesariamente estético. Puede
asociarse a él o no: es un sentimiento lógico que se relaciona con el estético
y puede producir un goce que se asemeje al placer de lo bello o que lo
sustituya, como sucede cuando se aprecian en una obra las condiciones
técnicas del artista solamente. El criterio es entonces reflexivo y no intui-
tivo. Es más lógico que estético. El espectador, sin cultura técnica, si bien
con cultura estética espontánea, no hace uso de ese criterio: intuye la
belleza al intuir la vida libre que expresa y se pronuncia sobre su valor
libremente, no en virtud de la sumisión a una norma" (p. 558).

resentaciones y ciertos actos del pensamiento, que no faltan nunca en otros movimientos del alma.[5] [Pp. 187–88]

## The Ugly

Deústua's discussion relating to the aesthetic senses clearly reveals that he could not accept Benedetto Croce's assertion that the ugly is exclusively limited to an "unsuccessful expression." Since Deústua admitted the existence of external representations in nature which give rise to feelings of harmony and freedom, he also readily accepted that the contemplation of what is inert, chaotic, detrimental, and useless can just as easily produce a negative reaction, namely, the feeling of the ugly. In both instances, neither is a purely willful creation devoid of any objective correlation. This does not imply, of course, that the articulated expression of an ugly object is unaesthetic. (Here, at least, Deústua would not quarrel with Croce that "every true intuition or representation is also *expression*" and that "intuitive activity possesses intuitions to the extent that it expresses them.")[6] But the converse relationship also holds true: the artistic rendition of an ugly object, however pleasurable its aesthetic attraction may be, does not render the thing itself, the subject matter, more charming. In fact, as an idealized version of nature—that is, as an insight into deeper reality—the artistic version should be uglier than the original. The aesthetic appeal, then, stems from another source. The viewer's aesthetic pleasure de-

5. Still, Deústua, for all his concern with the goal of art, occasionally failed to consider the vital role of the elementary aesthetic feelings. In the following passage, for example, he made intellectual feelings the determining aesthetic criterion: "El hombre así, no sólo resume, sino que, además, eleva a una categoría superior todas las perfecciones y, por lo mismo, todas las bellezas de la naturaleza, ofreciendo, junto con la belleza física y biológica, otros dos órdenes de belleza, la intelectual y la moral, que se inician débilmente en la actividad espiritual de los mamíferos superiores y que, en el hombre, llegan hasta crear, conscientemente, la belleza misma en el arte" (pp. 498–99).
6. Benedetto Croce, *Aesthetics* (New York, 1956), p. 8.

rives from his appreciation of another's inner, spiritual activity intuited on the viewer's part as an absolutely free activity: " . . . what gives us pleasure in that expression of the ugly is the soul of the artist who chooses freely the elements of his works and who arranges and combines them in harmony with his artistic ideas" (p. 280).[7]

## The Inferior and Superior Degrees of the Beautiful

To understand Deústua's distinction between the inferior and superior degrees of the beautiful, his conception of the beautiful must be further delineated, since the former is totally dependent upon the latter. As stated in the discussion of the ugly, Deústua is convinced that the determining factor of an aesthetic activity rests upon the working of the mind as it freely operates in the service of imagination, not of real fact and truth. When freedom finds the perfect order or harmony by which it is capable of expressing itself in a representation (an idealization of reality) it "reaches a superior state" (p. 375) and becomes an expression of the beautiful. The beautiful is that state where the imagination escapes the resistance of the external media through "a spontaneous or reflexive abstraction" (p. 375), creating or inventing an order or harmony that permits the most ample expansion of inner freedom. For Deústua, the word *graceful* captures the essence of the beautiful, since it effortlessly depicts the movement of life. Here inner freedom and nature are reconciled in perfect equilibrium, an ideal harmony begotten by the imagination. Deústua asserted, contrary to Kant, that this reconciliation between inner reality and external reality is "felt and not simply *per-*

7. This stand, it should be pointed out, obviously placed Deústua at odds with Croce once more. Croce saw the finished artistic product not as a sign of the artist's inner freedom, but rather as a sign of artistic liberation from impressions that renders the artist superior to them: "By elaborating his impressions, man frees himself from them. By objectifying them, he removes them from him and makes himself their superior. The liberating and purifying function of art is another formula of its character as activity" (*Aesthetics*, p. 21).

*ceived, real* and not *formal,* as Kant thought" (p. 382). As a
result, an object will be beautiful when: " . . . la *libertad* se
expresa por la *gracia,* que nace de una necesidad innata de
armonía con la naturaleza, como medio de alcanzar mayor
libertad, y que se resuelve en la armonía y la libertad del
sentimiento, como en la armonía, libertad y fecundidad de la
obra artística" (p. 382).

The feeling produced by the beautiful, therefore, is not a
simple one at all. Rather, it is one where sensible, intellectual, and moral values interfuse. Deústua maintained that,
notwithstanding its complexity, the feeling of the beautiful is
uniform and possesses a unilateral meaning. The beautiful
produces serene, completely pleasant, pure feelings in which
the reconciliation of inner freedom and order is realized both
in the object and in the subject. It is a reconciliation which the
senses perceive and the imagination grasps in a single harmonious act of intuition. In other words, the pleasant feeling
derived from the beautiful stems not only from the sum total
of the elements that make it up but also from the fact that each
individual component element (intellectual, moral, sensible,
associated, and direct factors) also gives rise to a pleasant
feeling in and by itself. In the various degrees of the beautiful,
this delicate equilibrium does not exist and consequently
weakens or exaggerates the aesthetic feeling. (It is imperative
to note that the division into inferior and superior aesthetic
feelings connoted for Deústua not a stepladder ascension in
aesthetic qualities, but rather the goal shot too short or over-
reached.) Undershot, it tends toward indifference and forms
the inferior degree of the beautiful; overshot, it leans toward
repulsion and forms the superior degree. In either case, however, the aesthetic content of the feelings involved prevents
them from becoming identified with indifference or repulsion
themselves:

Un estudio completo del fenómeno estético exige que se
comprenda, además, estas formas diversas, general-

mente consideradas como grado de superioridad o de
inferioridad; pero que en el fondo sólo son formas débiles
o impuras de lo bello, en las que los elementos de
libertad y de orden o armonía no ofrecen esa compene-
tración, ese equilibrio armónico de lo bello, sino com-
binaciones de otra índole, que debilitan el sentimiento o
lo exageran, haciéndolo fluctuar entre la indiferencia y la
repugnancia, sin llegar a confundirse con éstos. [P. 189]

In studying both categories of the degrees of the beautiful, it
should be noted that Deústua's previous discussion of aesthetic senses and inferior and superior feelings linked him with
the empiricist's approach to aesthetic sensations and put him
at odds with Kant's theory of the beautiful. Deústua asserted
that aesthetic feelings can arise from either within or without.
Internal origin strictly entails a creative mode stemming directly from the imagination; external origin admits to the fact
that things in bodily presence can and do concretely affect the
mind of the perceiver. Deústua thus tacitly denied Kant's
definition of feeling as that of a pure subjective sensation
completely independent of any object.

In discussing the degrees of the beautiful, Deústua recognized that he was sailing straight into the winds of subjectivity. Whereas his analysis of inferior and superior aesthetic
feelings allowed him to fall back on the objective studies
furnished by experimental psychology (compositional relationships and depth of content), his description of the inferior
and superior degrees of the beautiful lacked such objective
measures. Deústua, aware of the relative nature of his state-
ments, recognized that aestheticians split hairs over nuances
oftentimes hard to perceive. Furthermore, he acknowledged
that many designations are arbitrary and vague; that they vary
according to time, people, and place; and that to a great
extent they depend on the intellectual development of a
particular society. He endeavored to avoid unnecessary pit-
falls by probing only the most commonly accepted views

regarding the degrees of the beautiful. But his attempt to safeguard himself by limiting his inquiry to areas where a general consensus could be identified failed. The reason lay within the very nature of his postulates of freedom. As he himself pointed out in *Las ideas de orden y de libertad*, inner freedom can only be intuited; it cannot be rendered with any precision in discursive forms and it cannot be defined or distilled by reason. Its purely subjective nature never allows for objective verification. He accepted at face value a premise that can never be substantiated.

Deústua reduced the inferior degree of the beautiful to the general area of the "pretty" and the superior degree of the beautiful, in contrast, to the "sublime." The qualities associated with the words *attractive, gracious, enchanting, charming,* and *lovely* belong, for Deústua, to the inferior degree. He maintained that such designations refer to sensuous feelings produced by the "beauty of smallness in magnitude or quality" and to those which, corresponding to the initial moment of aesthetic emotion, principally "affect the senses" (p. 190). The common denominator among the inferior degrees would then be the existence of agreeable feelings, glass-plate reflections lacking spiritual spontaneity, fullness of life, or consciousness of inner freedom. In short, the inferior degree of the beautiful lacks qualitative and quantitative force. Accordingly, Deústua observed that the pretty discloses some sense of free life (if only weakly), and the lovely does so without much intensity. For their part, the attractive, the charming, and the enchanting produce pleasant feelings without encroaching upon the domain of thought. In the gentle, the delicate, the distinguished, and the elegant, Deústua contended, liberty appears simply as an easy, leisurely movement, albeit without characterizing the object. Graciousness goes one step further and renders free and expressive movement, but in so doing it reveals the effort and struggle involved in trying to produce its harmonious effect, falling short of the beautiful.

For a dedicated servant of spiritual and social freedom like Deústua, the pursuit of the inferior pleasures of the beautiful is without merit. With Kant, Deústua firmly believed that the work of art has moral and pedagogical implications. At best, then, the most harmonious combinations of expressionless forms or the richest combinations of sensations are only capable of "lifting the soul from the inferior level in which the senses delight in intoxicating the soul, but without creating anything, without producing that intimate awareness of interior freedom that characterizes the second movement of aesthetic emotion" (p. 199). Consequently, a predilection for any of the inferior pleasures—be it for the pure sensuous value or for the establishment of an aesthetic creed such as art for art's sake—constituted in Deústua's mind a sign of moral decadence, indicating estrangement from great art (with its ideals of freedom) and the triumph of the empty forms of decorative art. Alone, decorative art produces sensible and egotistical pleasures. It cannot, Deústua alleged, introduce man into the peaceful inner sanctum of the beautiful:

> Una sensibilidad extenuada por los placeres o halagada por las conquistas de la fuerza biológica, una sensibilidad refinada por el empobrecimiento de la vida o endurecida por las groseras satisfacciones del egoísmo, es igualmente incapaz de asociarse a ese esfuerzo de imaginación y de penetrar en el verdadero santuario de la belleza, en donde sólo son admitidas las almas sanas y vigorosas que, por un esfuerzo común de la razón y de la voluntad, se han hecho capaces de conocer profundamente la realidad y de elevarse sobre sus contradicciones y miserias hasta las regiones superiores del ideal. El goce intelectual de lo bello sólo se adquiere allí con plenitud. [Pp. 199–200]

The sublime (a superior degree of the beautiful) as opposed to the pretty (an inferior degree of the beautiful) is, for Deústua, a modality of the beautiful. Still, although the beautiful and the sublime are species of the same genus—that is, moments of the same feeling—they are significantly dissimilar. In contrast to the beautiful, where the self instantly captures the harmonious elements in the external object, the sublime provokes from the outset a mixed feeling of pain and pleasure. This bilaterality of feeling (significantly different from the unilaterally pleasant effect of the beautiful) stems from the numbing impact of the sublime object on man's senses and imagination. Before the sublime, the senses fail to perceive an objective order or pattern. By its very grandeur, the sublime presents itself in sensible forms of such unlimited proportions that it exceeds the power of identification by the senses and comprehension by the imagination. The senses cannot encompass or grasp the sublime because man inherently lacks any preexistent model with which he can identify the perception (apparent or real) of a great and overwhelming force. The sublime, then, leaves man's soul disturbed and dazed, too impotent to overcome and dominate the original state of anxiety and bewilderment it feels. The violence committed to the senses and to the imagination acquire an aesthetic character (that is, the sublime approaches the beautiful) when and if imagination imbues with a semblance of harmony that which ultimately must remain by its very nature indeterminate to the mind. Evidently, the sublime participates in the beautiful mediately, as opposed to the immediately or intuitively grasped aesthetic feeling of repose and harmony engendered by the beautiful itself. The aesthetic quality of the sublime stems from an apparent resolution of an incipient conflict which, through a concerted effort on the part of both reason and will, endeavors to bring harmony to an otherwise unrestrained burst of freedom. From a practical point of view, this implies that a work of art never depicts but only approximates the artist's feeling of the sublime. For, regardless of the technical mastery of an artist, one can hardly expect him to form a clear and coherent representation of that which in principle the imagination indefinably perceives.

*Feelings Generated by Tragedy, Comedy, and Drame*

In addition to the feeling of reverential fear and astonishment, Deústua posited that a strong moral element always accompanies the observation of any phenomenon that transcends the power of man's understanding. Thus the contemplation of the sublime in nature—for example, a tempest, the sea, the starry heaven—would conceivably work to curb man's egotism, since nature's limitless aspect would restrain him from glorifying and venerating his own finite individuality. Turning to the dramatic arts, Deústua claimed that this moral factor present in the sublime also constituted the very essence of tragedy. The tragic, if it is to exist, must combine a personal moral flaw with an overall sense of purpose under the sign of an inevitable and catastrophic outcome that remains at all times beyond human control. For to witness the destruction of a character caused exclusively by external circumstance would give rise to a sense of injustice. It would present man as an innocent and random bystander suffering to no purpose. On the other hand, destruction brought on solely by a moral flaw in character would suggest blatant criminality. A guilty act unconnected to any great external design could hardly provoke sympathy in a spectator. Consequently, only the destruction of something great, sublime in the human sphere of values, can possibly provoke the feelings of pity and fear. Moreover, in every case the conflict enacted supposes a struggle of the will and passions of a free soul against an outside, dark, incomprehensible force perceived as a blind necessity. From a historical point of view, classical tragedy, according to Deústua, stands as the paragon of the sublime, unveiling the battle and fall of an aristocratic soul before an irrevocable fate or an unbending sociopolitical order, whereas modern tragedy would constitute the model for contemporary man's crisis of conscience. In short, the objective mode of the sublime always entails a feeling of the tragic, since every instance involves the destruction of a great moral will by a more powerful moral or immoral force: "Cuando lo trágico representa la lucha heroica de la voluntad contra el destino inexorable, contra cualquier valor moral absoluto, sucumbiendo en esa lucha, el espíritu humano supera el nivel de la actividad ordinaria hasta convertirse en ilimitado en su poder, elevándose también a la categoría de un absoluto capaz de desafiar ese poder moral incontrastable. Lo trágico adquiere entonces el valor de lo sublime . . . " (pp. 488–89).

Deústua's foregoing discussion of tragedy and the sublime tacitly assumes that the psychological concept of aesthetic distance is critical to both the expression and appreciation of the sublime. Since the sublime cannot be the object of an exact representation of the mind, the mental or objective representation formed of the sublime must necessarily be once removed from the immediate feeling of the sublime as experienced existentially by the artist. In turn, the spectator of a tragic play finds himself twice removed from the original feeling of the sublime. Not only is the author's original response to this particular reality closed to the spectator—for Deústua, incidentally, tragedy, comedy, and the drame exist independently in real life—but the spectator's response to the incidents enacted on the stage relate to events that he has not in all probability experienced or perceived directly with such intensity. From the viewer's perspective, then, the tragic feelings of compassion and fear relate solely to the representation depicted objectively on a stage. As an observer he is conscious of the fact that the devastation of harmony or the destruction of a great ideal can never be identified with life itself.[8]

A similar presentation of an unavoidable conflict, which,

8. Here Deústua's views coincided to some extent with those expounded by Eduard Bullough, the English psychologist who ten years earlier had elaborated this concept in his article " 'Psychical Distance' as a Factor in Art and an Aesthetic Principle" (*British Journal of Psychology*, 5 (1912–13), 87–118. However, Deústua did not designate psychical distance as a universal principle of art. To the best of my knowledge, Deústua was not acquainted with Bullough's work.

in contrast, is only apparent or absurd, will be comic.[9]
Deústua maintained that freedom is just as fundamental an
ingredient to comedy as it is to tragedy. However, freedom
plays a different role in comedy than in tragedy. In comedy, it
does not succumb to superior forces; rather, it triumphs over
the contradictions of life and reestablishes harmony by
eliminating the pseudo-conflict. In spite of Bergson's overall
influence on Deústua's philosophic conception of life, it is
significant that Deústua opposed the point of view which
Bergson, in 1908, expressed in his book *Laughter*. Deústua
implicitly refused to tie laughter to Bergson's limiting concept
of the comical. Whereas Bergson conceived of laughter as
being solely on a utilitarian plane—that is, as a corrective to
human foibles—Deústua argued in favor of a multifaceted
origin.[10] Deústua insisted that laughter can be associated with
the beautiful as well as with the pleasurable, comical, serious,
painful, or ugly—that laughter can spring from an innocent,
sincere, bitter, violent, or malicious experience. He was convinced that Bergson's failure to recognize the complex nature
of laughter mistakenly led him to identify laughter exclusively
with the ridiculous. The latter, Deústua believed, springs
from scorn and is thereby a species of the ugly. Deústua
preferred to think of comedy more as entertainment dedicated to promoting the feeling of innocence and pure joy.
Thus freedom in comedy is a positive, nondestructive, and

9. The different forms of the comical, like the degrees of the beautiful, are highly subjective and, strictly speaking, indefinable. Deústua listed
the generally acknowledged ones: burlesque, or objective, comedy; witty,
or subjective, comedy; humoristic, or objective-subjective, comedy; high,
middle, and low comedy; benign and malicious comedy; and tragicomedy.
But he never dealt with them in detail (p. 252).

10. Although Deústua also stressed the intellectual and moral aspects
of comedy, he admitted that they are not what ultimately determines its
aesthetic feeling of liberty: "El factor cognoscitivo entra . . . en esta moda-
lidad estética . . . ; también es factor importante de su contenido la idea
moralizadora; pero estos elementos no determinan el sentimiento estético
de la libertad, aunque sin ellos, especialmente sin el primero, ese sentimiento no se realizaría" (p. 490).

playful reaction against what is serious in life. Man is supposed to enjoy life. He is not, Deústua affirmed, a creature destined only to suffer pain and sadness. His lightheartedness about what is somber, grim, severe, and solemn is a natural and, one is tempted here to conclude for Deústua, a spiritually healthy thing indeed: "Verdaderamente la seriedad, íntimamente sentida, no admite reacciones cómicas; el creyente no se ríe de los incidentes profanos en la Iglesia. Sin embargo, la reacción contra la seriedad es un sentimiento natural en todo hombre, que no está, por su naturaleza, condenado a la tristeza y al dolor" (p. 243).

However, it is in the drame,[11] characterized by "beauty of action" ("la belleza de la acción") (p. 252) that the feeling of beauty reaches its pinnacle in the dramatic arts. The drame differs from tragedy and comedy in that all human reality forms part of its scenario. Nothing need be left out. Its denouement, as a result, is neither tragic nor comic, although in content the drame contains both tragic and comic elements. Deústua emphasized that the drame, by portraying morally significant action and depicting character and situations with a degree of diversity and seriousness that is mirrored in real life, outstrips the other two dramatic forms in its potential affective content. Indeed, all the various and antagonistic situations brought together in a drame—for example, happiness-sorrow, pain-pleasure, hope-despair, aversion-love, serenity-anxiety, assurance-doubt—are potentially stimulating from both an intellectual and emotional point of view,

11. By the term *drame*, Deústua referred to the modern serious plays of the nineteenth and twentieth centuries that are neither regular tragedies nor melodramas. The French introduced the word *drame* to label the new type of domestic and social drama that developed in their country during the eighteenth century. This new form was "later introduced into England, where it is often called a 'drame'. It is a serious play, of which the modern *Problem Play* is an example" (William Flint Thrall and Addison Hibbard, *A Handbook to Literature* [New York, 1960], p. 158). However, since in English the word *drama* still retains an all-inclusive ring, I shall use the term *drame* for Deústua's allusions to the modern drama, in order to avoid unnecessary confusion.

since they form such an integral part of man's existence: "El sentimiento de lo dramático es el más accidentado y el más movido de los sentimientos estéticos porque no procede en una dirección, sino que se asemeja a un converger y a un entrelazarse de ondas cada una de las que adquiere intensidad mayor con el choque de las demás, sea por adición, como por repulsión" (p. 253).

*Humor*

Deústua averred that humor, unlike the comic, is essentially corrosive, abrasive, and nihilistic. Since humor is highly subjective in nature, it knows no thematic boundaries and allows for innumerable forms to convey its content. Humor can deliver its caustic sting in forms ranging from the pious smile to satire. All this makes humor inherently difficult to analyze[12] and also makes it next to impossible to determine objectively either the common or specific characteristics of humor. While humor exists in every generation, Deústua claimed that it is particularly prevalent during times of intense skepticism. During these periods of intellectual turmoil, attempts are made to raze established ethical standards of behavior and ideals of excellence and greatness. In this abortive process the humorist with his erosive vision, according to Deústua, plays a decisive role. Reducing with a vengeance all reality to the level of sheer appearance, the humorist's ironic attitude must also inevitably deride, disparage, and deny worth to society itself. Ultimately, then, humor plays havoc with human values, leaving in its wake cultural anarchy: " . . . el humorismo es obra de disolución en la

12. The overriding element of subjectivity explains its great variety and the humorist's absolute liberty to choose the medium best suited to his temperament and purpose. In Deústua's mind, this subjectivity also explains why vague attempts at classifying humor (for example, by nationality), always fail. Although in *grosso modo* one speaks of German, English, or Spanish humor, a critic, Deústua noted, would be hard put to explain how a single country such as England can produce such diverse types of humor as those of Shakespeare, Swift, Sterne, and Carlyle (p. 259).

cual predomina el sujeto como único poder moral, atri-
buyéndose un valor único ante el que los ideales objetivos
desfilan como entidades caducas, condenadas a la muerte bajo
el anatema de una ironía desdeñosa . . . " (p. 255). A verita-
ble saboteur of norms, the humorist with his damning humor
becomes, as it were, a negative God-figure or black angel bent
on destruction. On *terra firma* he is both an artist and a
skeptical philosopher and his product, humor, is also both
philosophy and art. As the following passage reveals, the
source of Deústua's views on this subject matter comes from
the Italian dramatist Luigi Pirandello:

> Hay así, en el fondo del humorismo, una profunda
> filosofía transcendental; no una filosofía abstracta del
> pensamiento, sino una intuición filosófica de la realidad
> vivida y de sus contrastes irremediables, que el positi-
> vismo superficial resuelve mediante hipótesis aventura-
> das, producto del deseo. "El humorista," como dice
> Pirandello, "es un poeta filósofo, que analiza la realidad
> toda con criterio de escéptico y pesimista, no para reír,
> con la risa del cómico, ni para indignarse, como el
> satírico, sino para negar todo valor objetivo de esa
> realidad y sonreír de los que creen en él." [Pp. 265–66]

## Superior Aesthetic Consciousness:
## The Artist, the Genius, and Artistic Creation

Up to this point Deústua had limited himself to discussing
aesthetic activity, namely, the contemplative moment dealing
with emotions experienced by those who partake of artistic
sensibility. Turning now to the other side of the aesthetic
coin, Deústua endeavored to analyze the act of artistic creativity, or that moment when aesthetic activity takes possession of
the artist's will and engenders the work of art. It should be
stressed here that for Deústua the act of creativity does not set
the artist apart from the rest of mankind as a superman. Yet he
is, to be sure, a person who lives and perceives life more

intensely and who, above all, has the technical ability or virtuosity to convert his aesthetic experience into a concrete work. To a certain extent Deústua recognized that heredity helps to explain the artist's ability to exteriorize his feelings. However, closer scrutiny reveals that sensibility, intelligence, and will, without which invention is impossible or sterile, clearly play a more fundamental role in the makeup of the creative faculty. Indeed, these faculties comprise the "original stamp" of the artist's "aesthetic personality" (p. 285); and it is the artist's temperament, influenced to some degree by the environment, that ultimately executes the work of art and brings it to its completion. The interaction between the subjective and the objective worlds, between the artist and his environment, produces a compenetration of the ideal and the real. The imagination continuously modifies reality, choosing and combining ideal and real aspects of reality "according to its feeling of love for freedom" (p. 286). Thus the reality imbedded in a work of art is, at best, an idealized form partaking of an ideal order.

Imagination, then, plays a key role in artistic creativity within Deústua's theory of aesthetics.[13] Without it there would be no artists.[14] Following the French psychologist

13. Deústua did not, however, underestimate artistic training. On the contrary, he readily admitted its importance but insisted that it can never substitute for natural talent: "Esa espontaneidad no es suficiente . . . para el desarrollo de las aptitudes del artista; se requiere . . . que sean cultivadas por una educación especial, propia del arte de su preferencia; porque en la creación de la obra artística, no sólo entra la invención, sino que . . . entran la rutina y la imitación. . . . Esta educación debe comprender al artista, como hombre y como profesional; debe ser . . . general y especial o técnica siendo ésta más importante que la anterior" (p. 290).

14. Neither Idealism, which stresses content, nor Realism, which stresses form, can alone account for the aesthetic phenomenon: "Sin la imaginación, la Idea no puede explicar el fenómeno estético, como emoción, ni como obra de arte; porque la tendencia de la Idea es de desprenderse de la forma sensible y adoptar la forma lógica del concepto, que aniquila la emoción estética. Sin la imaginación, la forma, tal como la entiende el realismo herbartiano, tiende también a convertirse en expresión lógica de relaciones, cuando pretende elevarse a sistema estético" (p. 546).

Théodule A. Ribot,[15] Deústua assigned to the imagination three constituents: the intellectual aspect that presupposes the negative operation of dissociation and the positive operation of association; the emotional, or impulsive, factor; and the unconscious factor often referred to as inspiration. This last is instantaneous and impersonal, not dependent on the individual will. But Deústua was reluctant to stop here. Alert to the possible deterministic implications of such a position, he endowed inspiration with a third characteristic—liberty: " . . . la inspiración, lejos de ser originada por la dominación tiránica de un poder exterior y superior al alma, como creían los antiguos, es, por el contrario, un desenvolvimiento más independiente y más libre del pensamiento humano y el triunfo temporal de una tendencia personal sobre las influencias antagonistas . . . " (p. 288). In fact, inspiration, guided by an ideal and propelled by strong emotions, liberates man from the routine of everyday life: " . . . (la inspiración) bajo la dirección de un ideal, desociando, asociando y sistemando elementos, y al impulso de una emoción vivísima, opera ocultamente y por sí misma, esa obra de libertad o de emancipación de la rutina, traducida por una forma nueva y superior del espíritu, inesperada para la conciencia" (p. 289). The nature of the imagination, depending as it does on temperament, will accordingly vary from artist to artist—hence the different styles within each medium and the different treatment within each style. Based on Ribot's analysis of creative imagination, Deústua classified the imagination into seven types: plastic, diffluent, mystic, scientific, practical-mechanical, commercial, and utopian. This arrangement permitted him to distinguish aesthetic from nonaesthetic activities, such as the economic, intellectual, and moral, and rendered the aesthetic activity as a self-encompassing and independent order.[16]

15. *Essay on the Creative Imagination* (Chicago, 1906).
16. The plastic and the diffluent imagination belong to the artistic order. The plastic imagination uses visual images above all and seeks to create sensory pleasure devoid of strong affective elements; it is

The difference between the artist and the genius is one of degree, not of kind, according to Deústua. It is determined by the superior forms of imagination or creativity.[17] Deústua rejected the pathological-physiological theories dealing with artistic talent and genius offered by Max S. Nordau because their scope of inquiry is applicable only to artists who are highly disturbed. Nor did he accept the positivist notions of such extremists as Taine and Spencer. Deústua contended that their theories dismally failed because they were based exclusively on the factors of race and environmental conditions. Although these factors are relatively constant for a given sector of the population, neither has produced geniuses in large numbers.[18] Deústua's own interpretation of genius, in turn, was a psychological one. It is evident that Deústua considers the genius an improviser, a man of intuition in whom inspiration—that is, spontaneity—not only predominates but constitutes the essential condition of his being. It would follow that, in such a man, the organization of ideas or of images is also spontaneously realized, without the long and tedious efforts of reflective thought. Nevertheless, Deústua did admit to a "directive idea," or ideal, engendered by inspiration. This ideal serves as a beacon, guiding the genius

---

characterized by clearness and precision of form. The diffluent imagination is the direct antithesis of the plastic one; it consists of vaguely outlined images that rely on suggestion and evocation for their effect. The predominating subjective element here, then, is emotion. Though opposites, both may fuse in one artist, as they do in Dante, Shakespeare, and Goethe. In all of them, "profound emotion" is united with an "intense and appropriate vision of reality" (p. 290).

17. Deústua distinguished sharply between genius and talent on a nonpractical level. Talent devotes its efforts essentially to imitation, to objective expression relying heavily on reflection (p. 302).

18. Although an antipositivist, Deústua was aware that the artist and genius cannot live outside of society. He readily admitted that the social climate influences the creator; he denied only that this fact has any deterministic implications: "Pero por individual que sea la creación, ella envuelve siempre un coeficiente social. En este orden ninguna invención es personal, en un sentido muy riguroso . . . " (p. 294).

in his attempt to give concrete embodiment to his inner vision. The "directive idea" is a complex state of mind, a composite of intellectual and affective elements. The intellect does not constitute an isolated function of this condition. Although the criteria of systematization and perception of relations found in nature are products of the intellect, still, for Deústua, the predominating aesthetic factor is volitional. In emphasizing this distinction, Deústua reaffirmed his belief that a work of art is something more than just a product of logical organization.

But even psychology, Deústua reluctantly conceded, cannot wholly explain genius. Spontaneity, in the last analysis, is an innate tendency, a breaking with the routine of everyday life. It is a force that strives to free man from external objects by modifying or reconstructing the outer world according to a profound subjective vision of reality. It is here that the genius parts company with the average man. The former adapts the objective reality to his subjective world and creates a new synthesis; the latter adapts his subjective reality to the demands made by the objective world. The very nature of the man of genius is thereby explained ultimately by his complete autonomy and individuality. Consequently, the true genius is a synthesis of liberty and harmony and not of harmony and technical dexterity: ". . . el genio . . . es *libertad* y *armonía;* el genio es libertad sistematizadora, que adquiere por la educación mayores elementos para satisfacer la tendencia a crear que resume su actividad" (p. 299).

## The Objective Characteristics of the Beautiful

Deústua rejected outright the possibility of an absolute standard of the beautiful. Three things coincide to preclude it: the relative nature of aesthetic activity, its dependence on human feeling, and its need to be manifested in a sensible form. The simple fact is that a single criterion of beauty—applicable to all art forms, to all periods, and to every country—has never existed. Aesthetic taste has been, is, and will be "as variable as it is uncertain" (p. 334). In fact, taste, or one's concept of beauty, has even varied within a given period or a given country. Deústua, however, was far from advocating anarchy in aesthetic judgment or taste. Although the objective characteristics of the beautiful—unity and variety—cannot aspire to become an aesthetic imperative determining artistic production, psychology has shown them to be indispensable to aesthetic pleasure.[19]

Interestingly enough, for all the emphasis that Deústua placed on form, he rejected the creed of "art for art's sake" just as vigorously as he refused to limit the aesthetic experience to one of pure content. Psychologically speaking, Deústua found form void of content unsatisfactory and consequently judged any work of art stressing pure form as an inferior product of art. Indeed, he denied the very possibility of "art for art's sake." In turn, to limit the aesthetic fact to content alone would also be detrimental to art, for it would tend to confuse the aesthetic phenomenon with morality: "Reducir la importancia del fenómeno estético al puro contenido, es confundirlo con el fenómeno moral, que puede restringir su acción al dominio del sentimiento puro; reducirlo a la forma, con indiferencia del contenido, es aceptar la fórmula del arte por el arte, una independencia que está contradicha por el análisis sicológico del sentimiento estético, que reconoce la solidaridad estrecha de todas las modalidades de la conciencia y el concurso necesario del elemento social en la génesis estética" (p. 545). Only when form and content are integrated

19. Deústua agreed that the elimination of form would negate expression and exalt absolute liberty. But in eliminating form, one has exchanged aesthetics for metaphysics. Without the sensible medium, then, the aesthetic phenomenon is crippled: "Puede la imaginación, al concebir un ideal, elevarse inmensamente sobre la realidad; pero, por grande que sea su elevación, el ideal no debe perder sus condiciones sensibles, su forma, para ser un ideal estético, ni perder su expresión externa para llamarse objeto bello. El carácter de perfección absoluta, extraño a toda limitación, no puede aplicársele . . . salvo que se prescinda de la expresión y se considere la libertad pura, la libertad en sí, como un absoluto; en cuyo caso, se sale del dominio estético para entrar en el metafísico" (p. 337).

does the work of art represent the expansive force of the spirit, that is, inner liberty.[20] And only then does it constitute a self-sustained whole whose beauty can be appreciated in and by itself without being related to another end, as usually occurs with functional or useful objects. For Deústua, the feeling of freedom—expressed through grace in its most perfect state—constitutes, then, the supreme moment of aesthetic emotion.

## Artistic Criticism

The gradual transition from aesthetic organs and sensations to objective embodiment of sensations in a work of art—with its implied use of aesthetic distance and the intervention of reason in, for example, the sublime and the humorous—comes to a full circle in Deústua's treatment of artistic criticism. For here the intellectual factor is predominant. Although in this respect artistic criticism differs widely from aesthetic activity, they have in common an initial contemplative stage. The critic's function is to grasp the "processes" of creative activity—that is, to imaginatively reconstruct the original composition and recreate the artist's experience as impressed upon his work—and to objectively pass judgment on the artist and his work. Postulating that a work of art is an expression of an autonomous act, Deústua nevertheless conceded that every artist is subject to influences, internal as well as external, during the initial period of artistic gestation. Deústua's ideal critic would consider all influences on the artist as well as the artist's "end" in creating his work and would delineate how "the free activity reflected in the artistic work" (p. 370) transforms the former into an original crea-

20. Consequently, it is only when the artist lacks technical ability to communicate his vision that one can separate content from form: "La separación sólo puede encontrarse, tratándose de las formas externas, que, no siempre, son capaces de traducir lo contenido en las formas internas establecidas por el alma entera, como sucede en las formas románticas del arte" (p. 545).

tion.[21] Clearly, Deústua did not see the critic fulfilling a normative role. Nor did he consider the critic the final authority on aesthetic matters. Since Deústua already recognized the relative nature of aesthetic taste and appreciation, the notion of either absolute utterances or infallible judges in the field of art criticism would have been, in principle, objectionable to him. At best the critic's view constitutes a working hypothesis, open to continuous modifications. The artistic genius, constantly breaking and creating new norms in his particular medium and steadily modifying the taste of his time (one could easily point to Pablo Picasso here to substantiate Deústua's view), can hardly be expected to adhere to the externally imposed rules of aesthetic criticism.

## THE PHILOSOPHIC PERSPECTIVE

The second half of *Estética general* examines the relations between aesthetics and other philosophic values. It scrutinizes in detail the aesthetic experience as a theory of knowledge; studies the possible connection between beauty and truth; differentiates aesthetic value from economic value; relates beauty to the good; and attempts to establish a hierarchy among the different arts based on the varying degrees of liberty inherent in each art form.

### Aesthetic Value and Activity

Delving into the creative function of the imagination, Deústua extended creative imagination to include the acts of the free conscious. Indeed, for him this is the most pro-

21. Thus Deústua rejected dogmatic criticism, or "idealistic criticism," which judges the work on fixed or absolute a priori standards. He rejected realistic, or scientific, criticism, which endeavors to reduce the aesthetic effort to a history of the artist's life, to a scientific study of his temperament, or to the establishment of a one-to-one correlation with his environment. And he rejects impressionistic criticism, which is based solely on the critic's sympathy for or antipathy to the product (p. 364).

found and the most essential function of the conscious. He criticized post-Kantian intellectualism for having converted aesthetics into either a metaphysical knowledge of beauty or a science of aesthetic phenomena.[22] He attacked that predominating order, essential to both logical and epistemological problems, for having given aesthetics independent status only as a "propedeutic of sensorial knowledge" (p. 407), identifying it with logic. And, as already stated, he vehemently denied that aesthetics concerns itself principally with logical order; rather, he asserted, the aesthetic order is a theory of knowledge wherein the spirit of liberty manifests itself in artistic imagery: "En la estética, como en toda la filosofía, se observa . . . el predominio de la idea de orden, aunque se comprende o, mejor dicho, se conoce por intuición, que el orden estético no es un orden lógico, destituído completamente de libertad, sino una armonía, en la cual late la libertad del espíritu bajo las imágenes que expresan la belleza artística" (p. 408).

Deústua observed that this intuitive knowledge was later confirmed when psychology became a positive philosophy of the spirit, scientifically investigating the psychic, sui generis phenomenon. For Deústua it was psychology, not reason, that illuminated the important role of the imagination in aesthetic creation. As spirit and imagination became synonymous, so did their corresponding activities, the "integral psychic activity" and "aesthetic activity" (p. 409). Hence, a theory of the imagination could lead to a true aesthetic con-

22. Deústua's attack was harsh. He asserted that intellectualism had obscured, not clarified, the nature of the aesthetic phenomenon: "En el desacuerdo en que permanecen todavía los sicólogos sobre la naturaleza misma del sentimiento, es lógico que el análisis del fenómeno estético sufra sus consecuencias y que, bajo el imperio subsistente aún del intelectualismo filosófico, que ha encontrado fuerte apoyo en la sicofísica, se persista en observar el fenómeno estético subjetivo, bien sea a través de sus símbolos expresivos e inmutables o bien con el instrumento de la experiencia científica, para descubrir leyes estéticas bajo la obsesión de la ciencia, que tiende a la inmovilidad de la vida" (p. 442).

ception "which . . . would be a true immanent theory of
philosophy, destined to render an explanation of all reality,
much the same as metaphysics aspires to do" (p. 409). Deústua believed that there were two reasons why such a theory
had not yet been formulated: the achievements of science had
encouraged an antimetaphysical tendency; and the idea of the
unconscious—which Deústua considered to be a pseudo-
scientific concept—finally seemed to resolve the question of
the subliminal activity of the psyche, which had always
haunted man and which neither rationalism, metaphysics, nor
theology was ever able to answer satisfactorily.

Still, Deústua's outlook on the psychology of the unconscious was not as negative as it seems. To refute this idea
absolutely, Deústua would also have had to refute Bergson's studies on memory and creative evolution on which
the theory of the unconscious rests.[23] Relying on contemporary psychology and Bergsonian philosophy, Deústua argued
against such intellectualists as J. F. Herbart, who speculated
that memory repeats exactly the perceived images deposited
in the unconscious. Rather, Deústua believed, it recreates the
image and its "virtual energy"; this creative function of memory is sheer imagination, and the whole spirit and imagination
explain both internal and external life: if the spirit could not
create "from the very start of its activity . . . " (p. 410), it and
inert matter would be the selfsame thing, in which case life
would not change or progress. Indeed, it would cease to be
life.

Deústua thus enlarged the aesthetic domain to include
any form of imaginative invention. The inartistic becomes that
which is repetitious, mechanical, or habitual; its effect is to
eclipse the conscious by an unconscious movement devoid of
liberty. What Deústua did, in effect, was to include "living

23. See Henri Bergson, *Matter and Memory*, trans. Nancy M. Paul
and W. Scott Palmer (London: S. Sonnenschein & Co.; New York: The
Macmillan Co., 1911), and *Creative Evolution*, trans. Arthur Mitchell (New
York: H. Holt & Co.).

reality" within the aesthetic realm. Furthermore, because aesthetic reality does reflect universal truths, it must be considered metaphysical in nature. In order to perceive art's role in every area of life, one must first study the creative imagination, whose essential characteristic is inner liberty. Thus, Deústua eliminated emotion as the determining artistic factor because emotion deters the "energy of the will" (which is responsible for the psychic synthesis of the imagination) from exercising "its creative action" (p. 457). Moreover, Deústua was convinced that a psychological study of the artist would show that the work of art is identical to "volition or immediate life, the exact equivalence of the conscious, of pure activity, . . . of the state of mind, of the ego in its plenitude, that tends to realize itself in its expansion without bounds" (pp. 457–58). This freedom of the creative spirit, which is clearly revealed only in artistic activity, is intuitively and immediately perceived and cannot be ascertained by scientific or logical analysis. For such analysis, in dissecting an object, destroys its unity or totality and therefore its liberty as well.

Consequently, aesthetics must be based on the notion of creative imagination if it is to become a "philosophy of the spirit" and not an "empty metaphysics" or merely a "science of phenomena" (p. 411). Deústua saw it rather as a new "immanent and transcendental metaphysics" (p. 411). Aesthetics must pinpoint, through data obtained from experimental psychology, the role of the image in the exercise of the creative function and the part it plays even in the animal's psychic life. For if to imagine is to construct with images, then all beings possessing senses—the instruments of perception— have the potential for creative activity. But aesthetics cannot stop here; it must go one step further. Taking the human imagination as its starting point, aesthetics must also endeavor to answer "the metaphysical problems posed by the hypothesis of a creative activity in nature and in God, [both of which are] superior to experience" (p. 411).

It should be noted here that Deústua only stated the above problems; he never expanded on them. He granted that aesthetics cannot hope to resolve queries pertaining to animal biology, much less tackle metaphysical issues per se. They simply go beyond the domain of aesthetic inquiry. Yet Deústua could not refrain from speculating on the metaphysical nature of creativity itself. He affirmed, following in the footsteps of Bergson, that aesthetics can conceive of a creative "faculty" whose creativity results only from "its own expansion" (p. 412), not directed toward any specific end. Moreover, he hypostatizes that aesthetics can even be conceived of as a "faculty that creates in virtue of an immanent end without the need of the senses, which do not engender that faculty, but which instead are its consequences and the immediate practical results of the creative activity exercised under conditions of resistance of adaptation to the medium" (p. 412). According to Deústua, the senses limit the intensity of this spiritual faculty in man; the intervention of the image never strips it of any of its inherent creative properties. Since this faculty unfolds, as it must, in nature, it freely fashions the image in harmony with nature herself.

To imagine, then, is to create, to undertake a free activity, to give birth to new elements and to new combinations of existing ones. Concluding that the fundamental characteristic of imagination resides not in the image but in the attendant feeling of liberty, Deústua equated imagination and spirit. In turn, the spirit's degree of creativity depends on its powers of concentration and expansion. In animal life one cannot speak of aesthetic activity, since the power of concentration leading to "self-awareness" does not exist. The animal's psychic life is one of pure objectification. In man the degrees of concentration and expansion vary from one individual to another. The result is an infinite variety of works produced by the imaginative, free-willful activity of the psyche. Given Deústua's aesthetic philosophy of the spirit, which he envisioned as a continuous creative activity, a good number of nonaesthetic human activities (like philosophy, science, and mathematics) would rightfully fall within the aesthetic domain. Liberty, the generating force of art, would make every soul artistic if nature did not coerce it. Free of restraints—that is, free of practical and utilitarian necessities and concerns that encourage habit-forming activities—every human action would be free and the free act itself would constitute a work of art. In such an act, the senses (and through them, consciousness) would intuitively receive the direct, profound impression of inner reality. Subsequently, imagination would embody this unique discovery of reality in either concrete or abstract form: concrete, if the object of the will "constitutes the most perfect [example of] individuality"; abstract, if it is "the most perfect [example of] universality" (p. 416). In either case, the artistic forms created spontaneously through the intuition of that inner reality are superior to those found in man's everyday "imperfect and deficient reality" (p. 415).

Briefly, then, the following terms are synonymous for Deústua: *spirit, imagination* (or *creation*), *art, liberty.* As he himself stated, "It is not possible to deny that imaginative and artistic function to the soul" (p. 415). Aesthetic form, consequently, is found wherever liberty is present. In Deústua's mind it was irrelevant whether liberty results from noncoercion or whether it exists as a figment of one's imagination, a mirage—as sensory illusion or forgetfulness. Liberty is that for which the soul yearns, the source of all its pleasure, even sensory pleasure. Deústua added that to replace liberty as the aesthetic value with any other—whether moral, logical, economic, or religious—is to deny the very existence and possibility of aesthetic phenomena. For in all other values, liberty is either conditional or absent. Without liberty, Deústua warned, one may have a social, religious, or economic product, but never art, never the beautiful.[24]

24. Still, Deústua recognized that although one can theoretically distinguish aesthetic from nonaesthetic values, one cannot logically conclude that the aesthetic phenomenon is present in a pure form. The aes-

92   Alejandro O. Deústua

*The Beautiful and the True*

Deústua recognized that the inherent vagueness and the open structure of language make it difficult to delimit ideas. Treated concretely, they can be clearly represented, but to deal with ideas on the abstract level can be perplexing. They tend to lose "precision and are susceptible to various interpretations and meanings" (p. 559). Confusion arises, for example, when one tries to discover the connection between truth and beauty. It would seem to be an easy task, if the content and extension of truth and beauty could be taken for granted. But Deústua found it painfully difficult to establish the similarities and differences between them.

Deústua based his distinction between truth and beauty on the content of the beautiful. In the latter "all factors of the conscious participate subordinated to that of freedom" (p. 565). As a result, all mental activities to some degree enter into the aesthetic act. This implies that aesthetic theory perforce includes the intellectual aspect as well. But to consider art as a logical product would be to commit the error of identifying art with the expression of empirical reality, of making art basically mimetic. Artistic movements such as realism and naturalism, for Deústua, were upshoots of this erroneous conception. On the other hand, when art saw itself as the expression of ideal truths, it too fell into a similar trap by taking on the task of imitating models that embodied or exemplified perfection. In both cases the function of art was limited to truth and to the creation of archetypes. This left little or no role for creative imagination.

The confusion of beauty with truth also blurs the distinction between art and science and the relationship between art

---

thetic phenomenon is not isolated from other social occurrences; in fact, it is closely related to them. Reality is far too complex to allow for the existence of pure activities. Furthermore, reality is necessary if liberty is to exist at all. For if the spirit is continuously striving toward a movement free of coercion, reality furnishes the stuff that provokes "the consciousness of the ego" (p. 438), spurring the spirit to free itself from the limitation it sets.

and philosophy. As has been noted above, the presence of the creative imagination for Deústua implies the existence of art in any sphere of human activity, including science. This is why he would surely have ascribed an aesthetic character to, for example, the non-Euclidean geometry developed since the turn of the century. Together with art, mathematics and science share such qualities as self-consistency, simplicity, precise organization of the flux of sensory subject matter, and the economic and emotional purport of obtaining the maximum effect for the least effort. Moreover, science and mathematics (like any other field of endeavor) have the same origin as art, namely, intuition. In fact, had Deústua been familiar with the works of Henri Poincaré, Ernst Mach, Richard Avenarius, and Hans Vaihinger he might have come to view the sciences differently than he did. He would have realized that the sciences are equally an invention of the mind, projections of the mind, forms of the mind, namely, artificial systems of signs created to handle the world of actual experience. Like works of art,[25] each system has its own inner rules as it seeks to organize into a coherent and self-sustaining whole the chaotic stream of impressions that endlessly bombard man's senses. According to these scientists, the arrangement arrived at does not reveal reality but serves as a convenient instrument to control it. The meaning of the symbols is in their use. The symbols themselves, they are careful to point out, are nothing more than fictions. The problem is that in science, man often forgets this point and treats these fictions as if they were the ultimate stuff of reality. In art, he never considers them anything but fiction.

But Deústua, unaware that these scientists had dealt a devastating blow to determinism, still held firmly to his

---

25. Subramanyan Chandrasekhar, one of the foremost contemporary astrophysicists, has noted (in the *University of Chicago Magazine*, 67, 4 [Summer, 1975], 4) that all scientists and mathematicians, in their own particular way, also quest after "the same elusive quality: beauty."

eighteenth-century concept of science and, like Bergson, fell into the trap of viewing science from a completely deterministic perspective. This explains why he was so adamant in maintaining that the imaginative function is not scientific, regardless of how creative the scientist himself may be. Deústua insisted that scientific knowledge is logical in nature and that it excludes feeling and liberty from its domain, subjugating "all phenomena to the rigorous determinism of [natural] law" (p. 576). As a result, Deústua's conventional view of science reconciled thought with reality and identified reason and science with mechanistic necessity. He thought of natural laws as real and existing, never as mere mental constructs.

Mistaken as he was on this score, Deústua was correct, however, in pointing out that science differs from art in the manner in which it interprets reality and in its teleological goals. Science seeks to understand objective reality through quantitative, abstract, universal relationships and finds its validity and value in verification and duplication. The validity of art, on the other hand, is purely subjective, individualistic, and concrete. The aesthetic moment and the art object are nonrepetitive, nonmeasurable, and nonpractical facts. Any given aesthetic moment and any given aesthetic product constitute an end-experience, an act of self-actualization that is characterized by disinterestedness, innovation, and spontaneity, which defy either mathematical or abstract analysis. Based on feelings and not on objective causal principles, art creates a relative order in the world of the imagination and reconciles reality with individual liberty. In other words, art harmonizes an individual's unlimited perceived inner freedom (consciousness) with the objects that tend to restrict it.

While sharp differences separate art from science, a marked similarity in content closely relates philosophy to art. Deústua argued that philosophy encompasses not just the intellectual but the complete life of the spirit. Its function is not to establish logical systems but to elevate inwardly the process of life, that which is most original in man, permitting him to contemplate reality with greater interiority and essentiality. This view of philosophy, according to Deústua, receives its highest expression in Bergsonian philosophy and "reflects the superior, sovereign nature of artistic creation" (p. 579), since it considers the free and omnipotent will as the most essential element of reason. Still, Deústua acceded to one fundamental difference between philosophy and art. Philosophy constructs its system not out of aesthetic consideration but because it holds it to be true.

## The Beautiful and the Useful

Deústua held with Kant that the aesthetic act is fundamentally a disinterested one, seeking nothing beyond itself. Economic pursuit, on the contrary, depends entirely on the imperative of desire, destroying the autonomous character of the act proper. Art and utility, however, may be interlaced during the moment of aesthetic conception and in the teleological purport of the art product. Deústua conceded that the final artistic creation may very well have had a utilitarian origin or that it may have been conceived for a specific purpose other than that of purely qualitative apprehension (for example, to heighten a religious experience). He accepted the idea that such objects can produce aesthetic emotion, provided they lose their external function at the moment of contemplation. To be sure, if the object itself is highly practical by nature (for example, a toaster), its aesthetic value would normally be of minor import; whereas in the case of less practical objects (for example, a religious painting or an urn), the intensity of the aesthetic emotion may suffer, but the beautiful is still present. Were one to eliminate liberty completely, only the economic factor would remain. Yet in one important aspect the beautiful is not totally disinterested for Deústua. In contributing to man's education and to his felicity, the beautiful "is of great usefulness and therein springs its *interested* and *interesting* character, in a higher sense than that found in the economic sense of the useful" (p. 607).[26]

## The Beautiful and the Good

While a sharp antithesis exists between the beautiful and the useful, the difference between the beautiful and the good is less apparent.[27] For liberty is a vital factor in ethics, as in aesthetics. Accordingly, Deústua contended that the moral ideal can be thought of as an aesthetic creation, and that the acts motivated by this ideal can be termed aesthetic. A deed of great moral value becomes a beautiful one, and the two qualities are so interwoven that it becomes impossible to separate them without destroying the effect of the action itself.[28] Yet the role of liberty in ethics is different from that in

26. Deústua cited architecture and oratory as proof of the compenetration of the economic and aesthetic values, where the former enhances beauty and the latter "renders utility more effective" (p. 435). However, Deústua admitted that they are capable of shedding their economic skin and of rendering strong aesthetic emotions: "El tránsito de lo útil a lo bello es tan insensible, y el cambio del uno por el otro se realiza de tal modo, que la arquitectura, arte principalmente útil, se llega a transformar en arte estético, que responde a un fin moral o religioso, que no tiene con la utilidad sino una relación muy lejana; la elocuencia abandona el fin práctico de convencer y agitar y se limita a producir emociones estéticas como el arte puro" (p. 610).

27. Aesthetic and moral emotions are closely connected when art serves a pedagogic function: "De esta confusión entre lo bueno y lo bello se ha derivado, en la teoría artística, el debate sobre la finalidad docente del arte; porque el arte no es sólo expresión de una libertad ideal, sino, también, proceso de liberación o de emancipación, encontrándose . . . y asociándose con la moral y la religión. . . . Este fin se ha conservado siempre; no sólo por los que han visto en el arte un poder ordenador de las energías síquicas, como los filósofos socráticos, para quienes lo bello es la regla moral, sino aún por los que han hecho de la libertad el carácter estético esencial" (p. 589).

28. However, if what is expressed does not pertain to the good, there is no aesthetic loss but only a loss of moral import: "No hay belleza moral cuyo contenido no sea una acción considerada como buena. Cuando eso no sucede, entonces la belleza deja de ser moral para convertirse en pura belleza artística" (p. 588).

aesthetics. The ethical act presupposes conscious abnegation, the real and free sacrifice of an impassioned and oftentimes legitimate impulse to a norm which the moral conscience considers superior and external to the will. Thus, for Deústua, the moral act contains within itself "the compulsion of duty" (p. 428), tied to a norm which subsists objectively, that is, externally and absolutely. Given the imperative character of the ethical norm—its "inevitable condition" (p. 428) —Deústua reasoned that the moral conscience feels the necessity of subjugating itself to the superior imposed order even when it may wish to rebel against the tyrannical decrees of this law. Liberty does not create this order, for if it did, Deústua noted, the ethical norm would soon lose the above characteristics and cease to impose upon human conduct a system of obligations.

In contrast to ethics, there are no absolute norms in art, nor can there ever be. Instead, there is the order created by the infinite liberty of the imagination, the free creation of the ideal which, for Deústua, "is everything." The existence of imperatives is, if not impossible in art, then at least created by liberty. Indeed, the surest sign of a great work of art is precisely its originality, and the genius (as has already been noted) can alter or destroy the existing norms and replace them with new ones at will. If, however, traditional artistic norms are followed, they are adopted freely because they are useful in producing the work of art. In brief, whereas the ethical ideal lies in universality, the aesthetic ideal lies in diversity; whereas the moral act is founded on the "inhibitory power of the conscience" (p. 429), the aesthetic act is essentially expansive; and finally, whereas moral pleasure is based on the comparison of the event with a precept that nullifies intuition and exalts reflection, aesthetic pleasure stems from the contemplation of the inherent quality of freedom posed by the event and in the sheer "intuition of the ideal" (p. 429).

*The Beautiful and the Religious*

Of all phenomena dealt with so far, Deústua considered the
religious phenomenon the most closely related to the aesthetic one.[29] In fact, they merge within the realm of "pure
ideality" (p. 597), or mysticism. For here, as nowhere else,
liberty (imagination), coming in contact with the absolute,
with the suprasensible realm of existence, discards all rep-
resentational forms. More significantly, Deústua observed
that art and religion, springing as they do from the same
source (mythology), have never really parted company. Religion has always turned to art to give concrete form to its
beliefs.[30] This did not blind him to the great difference between the two. The divine inspires religion: through the
religious state of pure feeling the divine seeks the nullification
of the self within the Absolute Being. Consequently, the
governing notion in religion is the norm dictated by the divine
will and apprehended through revelation. While liberty in
religion does lead to emancipation from external reality, it
also entails what is most offensive to Deústua, namely,
the submission of the self to a divine—that is, external—
principle. In contrast, art finds its ideals in both nature and
man and seeks to preserve the self through representation and
concrete works. The aesthetic state is thereby one of absolute
inner liberty exempt from any imperative that can either
impair or delimit inspiration, the work itself, or aesthetic
enjoyment.

29. Indeed, Deústua asserted that the most elevated aesthetic pro-
ductions have always had a religious theme. He cited as examples temples,
statues of gods, religious paintings, music with its "mystical profoundness,"
and lyric poetry "as a revelation of what is divine in the depths of the
soul . . . " (p. 437).
30. Deústua established a necessary relationship between religious
feeling and art. In fact, the former could not exist in man's conscious
without forms supplied by the imagination: " . . . el sentimiento religioso
no surgiría en la conciencia humana si la idea mística no se revistiese de
formas producidas por la imaginación y no se purificaría si esas formas no
fuesen idealizadas por el arte" (p. 437).

*Classification of the Arts*

The artist's existence, anchored in conscious life itself, is, according to Deústua, totally free; and his product, reflecting a deeper layer of reality than usually meets the common eye, arises from a disinterested creative impulse. Since the imagination is creative and free, nature alone, although it is often beautiful and at times even sublime, cannot satisfy the needs of an artistic soul. The artist feels the need to create, the urge to objectify his spiritual freedom in forms that will transcend the appearance of harmony which nature readily offers him. This superior reality, conceived by the artist, acquires through art an independent spiritual life. Deústua considered this spiritual life an indirect, secondary creation of nature because it is a product of the conscious wherein "creative life is transformed into creative spirit" (p. 508). Consequently, the work of art is not just a continuation of nature; it is also the final stage aspired to by the creative mind. In penetrating nature, the spirit does not create the beautiful as a reconciliation between nature and itself. Rather, the beautiful is the continuation of life's creative activity, which permeates the universe. Nature, which Deústua envisioned as representing life, must thereby always favor the aesthetic experience. The latter, in turn, furnishes man with a more direct, pure insight into reality and allows him to capture, for a limited time, life's immateriality in a vision that is free of utilitarian concerns. Thus considered, the aesthetic experience, lodged firmly in the conscious, is complete unto itself—indivisible from the individual spirit that creates it—and renders any aesthetic classification of said experience invalid.

The same, however, cannot be said of the different art media through which the aesthetic experience of the creative imagination is objectified. Deústua held that one can speak of aesthetic hierarchies among the arts, to the extent that they more or less delimit the complete concrete realization of the subjective expression of the aesthetic experience. It is an

intriguing paradox that Deústua, a devotee of Bergsonian irrationalism, followed Hegel's aesthetic hierarchies presented in *The Philosophy of Fine Art.* Bergson's philosophic
stand led him away from anything that would congeal duration, that would freeze and render inert the ever constant flow
of life. Matter and space, the annihilators of the Life Force of
the universe, arrest the creative free process of Real Duration, which ultimately is embodied in God by Bergson. To
accomplish this end, logic and reason become tools of utility.
Ideas obscure and disfigure reality. Language, as a result,
cannot adequately convey reality since, at its core, it com-
municates in conceptual terms. In this practical, linguistic
world, the poet is the exceptional man who, as a stranger
inhabiting the earth, focuses his attention on Real Duration
and reveals his communion with the fluid stream of life in
works that break, albeit briefly, with language's basic function
as a medium of utilitarian expression. Words, as a rule, do not
help to discriminate qualities. They class them and designate
*genera.* By circling around the object, words describe its
practical and convenient facets without ever rendering or
presenting the object itself. The poet, then, does violence
to language. He deliberately misuses language—indeed, his
words are a species of catachresis—to reveal unique essences
perceived in a unique time by a unique state of consciousness.
The words that stream from a poet's pen express what language was never meant to express. If pressed, Bergson would
relegate poetry to a comparatively low aesthetic plane because of the natural ambiguity and circuitry of terms that the
poet must employ.

If the mind renders the most indirect or feeble of the
aesthetic experiences, then the perception of the object itself
is captured only through the senses. Of these, Bergson considered vision and hearing primarily as the aesthetic senses,
with hearing being the more intuitive of the two (ultimately,
vision and its correlate plastic art demand the spatialization or
freezing of life). Consequent to this view, Bergson placed

music above all the other arts as the most immediate and directly felt of aesthetic presentations. Through the ordering of sound and rhythm, music renders movement itself.

Hegel, in turn, classified the arts according to their dependence on material media and their proximity to conceptual expression. This led him to rank poetry first among the arts, with music and the plastic arts taking second and third place, respectively. Deústua, recognizing that technical dexterity is fundamental to artistic creativity and that the medium—as Lessing had stated in the eighteenth century—limits to a certain extent the artist's ability to objectify fully his intuition of reality, accepted the Hegelian classification. Even music is dependent on its medium (sound waves produced by instruments) for its effect and thereby leaves the perceiving mind once removed from the embodied work (the musical score proper). Only literature, of all art forms, frees man from the external media and places the work of art directly within the confines of the imagination. Thus, with Hegel, Deústua classified the arts in the following ascending order: architecture, sculpture, painting, music, and poetry.

According to Deústua, architecture is the artistic expression "of the inorganic, of the inert" (p. 511) and ranks as the lowest art form because, among the arts, it is the most mechanical. In architecture, the beautiful expresses the intellectual pleasure and the triumph of the free will in its struggle against the forces of gravity, the great regulator of the material world. Architecturally, then, lightness is always a "pleasurable," aesthetic quality. With Friedrich von Schlegel, Deústua called architecture "frozen music" (p. 512). The analogy is based on the harmony of relations that can be reduced to numbers in both media. Deústua claimed that the architectural beauty of a building does not lie in its formal qualities. Rather, it stems from the building's "material equilibrium" (p. 512), fostering in the observer a sense of liberty obtained through its static rhythm or its ascensional movement.

Whether or not a structure can be judged artistic depends

in some measure, for Deústua, on the external end for which it was conceived. With respect to Egyptian, Oriental, and Indian architecture, Deústua refused to grant them artistic value on the grounds that their respective societies viewed them exclusively as a "revelation of religious feeling" (p. 412) and not as works of art. Rivaling nature in their monumental massiveness, these colossal signs stand as symbolic representations of mythological beliefs subordinated, on the one hand, to religion with respect to their significance and, on the other, to the science of construction with respect to their structures. The emotion expressed by such temples and tombs (for example, the Egyptian pyramids) is one of "magnificence," not necessarily one of "sublimity." The amazement provoked by their contemplation, Deústua insisted, is unaesthetic because both imagination and individuality, namely, the stamp of a particular creative conscious, are absent.

> La emoción que producen esas grandes masas, que sirven de templos o de tumbas, es la de lo *grandioso*, que no siempre se convierte en lo sublime. . . . Ellas pueden conducir a la meditación de las energías consumidas en esas obras, que suponen duraciones inmensas y abarcan espacios considerables; pero el asombro que de esa meditación puede resultar, no constituye un sentimiento estético, mientras que la imaginación no encarne, en un espíritu libre y poderoso, el centro motor de esa materialidad desmedida; en cuyo caso, el valor estético estaría en esa creación imaginaria, no en los elementos que la habían sugerido, expresivos todos de la inercia. [P. 513]

Interestingly enough, Deústua also insisted that the above criterion does not hold true for either classical architecture (the Hellenic temples), or romantic architecture (Gothic, Moorish, and German structures of the Middle Ages). He contended that these are highly artistic in spite of the fact that they always retain their utilitarian function. In the case of classical architecture, equilibrium or static rhythm gives the Greek temple a eurhythmic sense of organic life, creating the emotional effect of a mass capable of liberating itself from the enslaving force of gravity and of reflecting the harmonious and tranquil soul of its people. This emotional sense of freedom, Deústua added, is witnessed to an even greater extent in the Gothic cathedral. Here it is produced by the freely upward-soaring form, symbolizing man's ardent spiritual life, unrestrained by rational limits and ascending to heaven in mystical flight.

Turning to sculpture, Deústua held that it acquired aesthetic form only during the Athenian Golden Age. For it was then that the rigid inexpressiveness of the architectural and hieratic statuary of Assyria and Egypt was overcome and transformed into a living art under the Greek ideal of free life. With the Greeks, sculpture reconciled repose with free movement and rendered a lifelike impression to matter. This gave birth to the fusion of "the soul and life" (p. 514), which in the classical conception of beauty was envisioned as a static expression suggestive of dynamic emotion. But sculpture, for Deústua, obviously cannot stop here. Deústua emphasized that sculpture needs to surpass this ideal of harmony and to strive toward a greater synthesis of both physical and moral life. It must express that state of self-awareness of the inner life of the soul, foreign to Hellenic life, which characterized Occidental society after the advent of Christianity. According to Deústua, the foremost representative of this new Weltanschauung, the artist who depicted the soul in its most complete state of self-concentration, was Auguste Rodin. Rodin's sculpture interprets and renders spiritual states through mass and lines. His work awakens in man the feeling of eternal duration and of infinity through the use of colossal figures that triumphantly portray the will of heroism and intense psychological drama. Sculpture thus can reveal a profound intuition of life in its totality and become, as in Rodin's meditating figures, the sublime symbol of humanity.

Painting alone among the plastic arts comprehends both architecture and sculpture, since it encompasses the entire physical and psychic reality. However, painting differs from the other two in that it renders the actual objective shape—the material reality of forms—into an artificial illusion or artistic appearance. In its ability to express readily man's subjective experience through the medium of color exclusively, painting (like music) has as its subject matter "pure feeling" (p. 516). The very nature of color nullifies any notion of weight, so characteristic of both architecture and sculpture. Reality in painting becomes nothing more than a colored surface that vividly suggests not only physical but, more importantly, psychic dynamism. Consequently, it comes as no surprise that Deústua's pictorial ideal should be embodied in the dynamic, romantic concept of freedom. Painting, then, ideally pursues the superior order of the life within, that of spiritual substance, so that it may elevate man's soul above the external, finite, sensory reality. Forever searching for the infinite, painting touches the sublime "in heroism and sainthood, in the symbolic expression of the divine" (p. 517). The latter, however, springing from the internal life of the artist, always constituted for Deústua the exclusive products of the painter's imagination and never, as Hegel would have it, aspects of the "infinite concrete universality, under the guise of sensuously concrete form."[31] It is precisely this subjective factor, moreover, that serves as the criterion for aesthetic evaluation of pictorial beauty. This holds true even when a picture lacks any moral value whatsoever, as in the case of a still life or a landscape. Even such works, through the symphonic use of color, reflect the painter's imagination on the canvas as a creative—and therefore totally free—force.

Music, in turn, replaces the apparent free movement, the dynamic physical and psychic reality obtained through color in painting, with "the reality of that movement" itself (p. 518).

31. G. W. F. Hegel, *The Philosophy of Fine Art*, trans. F. P. B. Osmaston (London, 1920), 1, 107.

Perceived solely in time, the sound waves of music completely destroy the visible form so vital to architecture, sculpture, and painting. More than any of the plastic arts, music (through tone) expresses feeling directly and fully, precisely because it does not have to contend with spatial dimension or with the conditions of space. One can hardly speak of inertia; for matter, as it were, has now become spiritualized. Outside of the ear that captures tone at a specific time, the sensuous medium of music does not enjoy external independence as does, for example, a building by Frank Lloyd Wright, a sculpture by Michelangelo, or a painting by Joseph Turner. Vanishing as quickly as it is perceived, tone lingers on or persists for long periods of time simply in memory. It is in this sense that Deústua argued that music exists exclusively in consciousness, in mind's imagination. He concluded that the activity required to retain tone—taking place as it does within the imagination—is, from the very outset, necessarily creative, which is also to say free. In Deústua's opinion, then, music's ability to interpret and create profound psychic states, to simultaneously communicate the subtle dynamism of moral life, feeling, and thought, is inherently greater than that of all the plastic arts.

Deústua's hierarchy of the arts closes with his statement on poetry or literary art. From the foregoing analysis, it becomes self-evident that Deústua considered poetry superior to all the other arts. He asserted that poetry, in contrast to the plastic and musical arts, does not rely on any external, sensuous medium to externalize imagination's affective state. The sound of a word serves exclusively as a sign or as a reinforcement of a sign, lacking independent value or substance in and by itself. Obviously, Deústua recognized that the word does possess a physical medium. His decision to disregard this fact was, therefore, not accidental but deliberate. However, his resolve was not based, as in Hegel's case, on any rationalistic attempt to identify the word with the work of an intelligence set on disclosing the manifestations of a universal Reason or Spirit. Rather, like Shelley, Deústua firmly believed that in literature, the medium is totally transparent and the medium and content are one with creative imagination. The uniquely inspired imaginative idea—the poetic word—is consequently the most perfect form in which an individual can actualize the expression of his self, of his inner freedom. And since the poetic word, relating the deepest feelings of the human soul, is completely inseparable from pure imagination, when grasped it can only be grasped by another imagination directly. In this manner, the contemplator who vibrates to the lyrical revelation of another's dynamic self, himself participates—without necessarily reduplicating the original psychological experience that led to its realization in the poet—in a creative act, an act of absolute inner freedom. What predominates in poetry is lyricism, since only the latter allows for the expression of "the value of the self, the value of free will in action" (p. 533). Here, then, Deústua differed radically with his mentor Bergson. Bergson was convinced that the poetic word must necessarily betray itself and congeal, kill the flow of life, because even the poetic word by its very nature cannot escape from the conceptual realm: words are mediated to the aesthetic experience, giving rise to images—a once- and, at times, twice-removed stance from the object—instead of revealing the actual movement of the life experience. Deústua claimed that, if anything, just the opposite is true. Man is at his best when he commands imaginative language. Man is truly himself when he is the imaginative word incarnate.

Obviously, the above poetic views of Deústua are in all respects romantic. But it should be underscored that by the term *romantic* Deústua was referring to a state wherein the artist searches not outside of but within himself for the content of his art. Deústua's criteria of a romantic poet are universal, with chronological time meeting defeat at the hands of inner time. Poets of any age, then, can belong to this spiritual guild as long as their works constitute the profound expression of consciousness and unveil the liberty of inner life.[32] Seen from this perspective, liberty and art go hand in hand with social solidarity and love; together, liberty and art constitute the unbreakable bond of man's faith in his fellowman: "El criterio de la libertad es, pues, el criterio estético,

32. Within this frame of reference, classical literature did not meet Deústua's criteria for lyric poetry. Deústua contended that Hellenic lyric poetry lacked independent form. Lyricism, whenever present, was always incidental, according to Deústua. Perhaps occasionally a poet would venture to pen his inner mood, but generally, for the Greeks, lyric poetry was choral poetry, accompanied by music, song, and dance. Since the main purpose of poetry was to celebrate mythological religion in cultural festivities, it could hardly be guided by those feelings awakened by personal hate, love, fear, or happiness. Deústua maintained that mythology, for both poet and plastic artist, was the ideal mirror of human life, reflecting the spiritual characteristic of the Hellenic race. Stressing harmony and equilibrium over feeling, artistic liberty in classical literature was limited to the formal or external facet of the poem, namely, style and language. Thus Deústua claimed that the Greek poet rarely, if ever, confided his inner self to his public. What he did was to rejuvenate a limited number of ideas then prevalent in verse: El lirismo griego no dependía, pues, como el moderno, de la musicalidad del espíritu, expresado por los sentimientos más profundos. . . . No era el sentimiento el factor esencial y dominante, sino la idea contenida en el verso, el elemento racional, objetivo, que debía mantener su claridad de expresión en medio de ese consorcio" (p. 527).
With regard to classical dramatic poetry, Deústua viewed it essentially as an art form directed by logic and geared to the universal order of ethical questions: "La armonía purificadora del desenlace [of tragedy], la *catarcis* griega producía un sentimiento de valor moral y aun de valor lógico, como una consecuencia racional de los factores en oposición; pero esos sentimientos extra estéticos, en sí, se asociaban al estético de la lucha libertadora, que producía un desastre. Para el espíritu helénico, enamorado de lo objetivo, esos factores extra estéticos, símbolos de una armonía realizada, tenían la más elevada importancia. Así se explica el carácter pedagógico de las estéticas de Platón y Aristóteles" (pp. 529–530). In contrast to the nonlyrical nature of classical literature, Deústua cited Dante (and Milton, surely, would also have been on his list) as a prime example of a romantic poet: "La epopeya dantiana es lírica; en su desarrollo atraviesa el mundo pictórico del infierno para hacerse musical en purgatorio y especialmente en el cielo que inunda de armonías y melodías musicales. El alma de Dante es de un profundo lirismo. Su carácter está determinado por la voluntad libre ante la que sacrifica todo otro bien. El lirismo, por fin, es musical aun en sus descripciones y narraciones; la objetividad se encuentra sometida al sujeto sirviendo de símbolo de sus anhelos" (p.533).

porque la belleza en su más amplia acepción es esencialmente libertad. "El verdadero arte es la libertad más elevada," dice Wagner. Y como la libertad no puede desarrolarse sino dentro de una solidaridad que es amor, la libertad y el amor deben edificar el arte" (p. 533).

# 5. Final Observations

Together with the Uruguayan Carlos Vaz Ferreira, the Argentinian Alejandro Korn, and the Mexican Antonio Caso, Alejandro O. Deústua must be considered one of the founders of contemporary philosophic thought in Latin America.[1] Above all, Deústua was a pedagogue and a thinker who found the necessary leisure to formalize his ideas only after he had retired from his academic career. Among those of his generation, Deústua was the only philosopher who eschewed religion (unlike Caso, who embraced Christianity in his writings); steadfastly organized his material under a unitary, cohesive theme (unlike Ferreira, who preferred to present his ideas aphoristically); and unswervingly identified the will with creativity (unlike Korn, who stopped short at will and freedom), developing the latter into an extensive philosophy of art. Although all four men perceived the important role which contemporary psychology had played in understanding the conscious as duration, Deústua was alone in recognizing its full impact on aesthetics. He was, in the Spanish nations of South America, the sole aesthetician of his time. He was also the only philosopher among his coevals who before 1925

1. Sánchez Reulet, p. 13.

rigorously applied the results of voluntarist psychology to defend the principle that human existence and creative imagination were one.

Yet, aside from these differences, all these figures shared one fundamental trait. Theirs was the voice of protest in Latin America when the continent was still riddled by positivist thought. After Gabino Barreda raised Comte on a pedestal in Mexico, positivism became the ruling political creed of the Porfirio Díaz regime for thirty-five years. In Argentina, Comte's views carried even more weight. In Mexico, Caso, Alfonso Reyes, and José Vasconcelos were at least able to steer the country into the new currents of idealism after 1911; but men like Victor Mercante, Leopoldo Herrera, Rodolfo Senet, and Alfredo J. Ferreira managed to keep Argentina and Uruguay under the narrow horizons of positivism until 1920. As late as 1924, their influence could still be felt as, under the direction of Ferreira, they formed the Argentinian Positivist Committee.[2] Korn, who was to become the most important and influential philosopher in Argentina by 1930, tried to reverse this trend and guide his country toward a philosophy of values.

Peru did not fare much better than its sister nations. When Peru finally emerged from intellectual emaciation and broke away from the stultifying constraints of positivism, it was under the driving force and spiritual vision of Deústua. The standard-bearer of individualism, Deústua realized that positivism logically purported the total annihilation of man. Positivism denied man the liberty to formulate the state of his mind. With the expression of the self denied, with man's self-dignity and humanity brushed aside, man could conceivably become a programmed cell with a conscious made to order.

Against this backdrop, Deústua rose and challenged the

2.  Juan Carlos Torchia Estrada, *La filosofía en la Argentina* (Washington, D.C., 1961), pp. 182–83.

positivists on their own grounds. He was convinced that the Comtians erred in thinking that material progress was synonymous with liberty. Liberty, Deústua proclaimed, was a psychological fact, not a material one. Man had to be free from within, he had to will himself free before he could be free. He had to recognize, cultivate, and extol the humanity of the human community before he could hope to be admitted to its fraternity. To counteract Comte's version of liberty, which subordinated liberty to the rigorous and invariable laws of nature, to rectify the deleterious effect which positivist determinism had had on his countrymen, Deústua propounded an aesthetic conception of human conduct based on the canon of spiritual liberty and disinterestedness. Only the aesthetic value, Deústua insisted in *La ley de instrucción,* allowed for the unimpaired continuous creativity of the soul; only the aesthetic value freed the soul from compromising with an external, superior, restrictive source. Neither subservient to religion nor state, but rather as a free agent, man would lead society toward real progress, namely, liberty itself.

Deústua's conception of art, accordingly, rendered repugnant to him the very thought that art should be either subject to or the expression of the state. (In this respect, Deústua would undoubtedly place Hegel, Comte, and Marx under the same roof.) There can be no authorized beauty within art's frontiers; there can be no state-authorized usurpation of man's consciousness or will. Herein lay Deústua's strong attraction to both Wundt and Bergson. Both exalted consciousness as a creative, free process and envisioned life as a continuum in which the self is fully realized. The creative flow of life, man's creative psyche, bathes everything with the uniqueness of personalized time. Creative consciousness apprehends the world in its radiant newness because it itself is always being renewed. (Like the hummingbird, the conscious never ceases in its flight, although it may mark time to draw the nectar of a flower that has caught its fancy.) Creative consciousness leaves stale, habit-worn visions behind to delight in the singularity of an object touched upon in an exclusive, nonexchangeable, irreversible instant in mind's time.

Deústua's subsequent works assiduously underscored this world view. They reinforced the belief expressed in *La ley de instrucción* that liberty is the only viable alternative to a mechanistic existence, namely, a form of life which decreed the survival of the fittest. After struggling for over two thousand years against theodicies, reason, and scientific determinism, psychological liberty, at the dawn of the twentieth century, had finally made its unmistakable imprint on Occidental culture. In his treatise on order and liberty, Deústua captured this birth and hailed the new era that pays tribute to the artist who is hidden in every man. Aesthetic contemplation would bring out the best in man because it would rid him of utilitarian concerns. The creative urge would foster, necessarily, an ethics based on altruism. The work of art, a completely gratuitous act of communication, would be accepted, in turn, as a product of true human magnanimity.

*La ley de instrucción, Las ideas de orden y de libertad,* and *Estética general* are therefore a call to arms. Deústua wanted man to think of himself in universal terms and not simply in a narrow nationalistic sense. He desired that his fellow countrymen, through aesthetic education, become optimists of life and citizens of the world. He wanted man to accept, admire, and defend life as a creative act, as an act of love, as a vital process imbued with dignity, truth, justice, sincerity, and tolerance. This is why in *Estética general* Deústua proclaimed poetry—the art of the human word which, for him, has no medium save that of the creative imagination—to be the highest expression of mankind. (This is why he would never agree with Bergson's extreme position that the word constricts and ossifies the very flow of life.) Deústua's aesthetics exalts that which is fresh and innovative in every soul. It tells those who would listen to accept man's creative works in all fields of endeavor as signs of social solidarity. For Deústua, aesthetics is and shall always be a theory of metamotivation.[3] Deústua's aesthetic philosophy is, in the last analysis, a philosophy in defense of man. No man, stated John Donne within a religious context, is an island unto himself. Deústua would assert that man is what he is not insofar as he is in God, but only insofar as he belongs to the whole of the human race.

3. The phrase *theory of metamotivation*, so applicable to Deústua, is taken from A. H. Maslow, *The Farther Reaches of Human Nature* (New York, 1971), part 8, pp. 299–340.

# Bibliography

WORKS BY ALEJANDRO O. DEÚSTUA

*A propósito de un cuestionario sobre la reforma de la ley de instrucción.*
Lima: Imprenta M. A. Dávila, 1914.
*Apuntes sobre la enseñanza secundaria.* Lima: Imprenta Americana, 1908.
"Apuntes sobre la teoría del valor." *Mercurio Peruano*, 11, 61–62 (1923),
39–46.
"Clasificaciones estéticas." *Mercurio Peruano*, 5, 26 (1920), 91–103. Re-
printed in *Revista de Filosofía* (Buenos Aires), 7, 5 (1921), 260–71.
*Cultura política.* Callao: Empresa Editora de "El Callao," n.d.
"El deber pedagógico del Estado." *Revista Universitaria*, 2 (1913), 487–
500.
"El dualismo en el problema pedagógico," *Revista Universitaria*, 2 (1913),
301–11.
*El problema de la educación nacional.* Callao: Empresa Editora de "El
Callao," 1905.
*El problema universitario; la cultura universitaria en Suiza.* Lima: n.p.,
1927.
"El valor estético." *Mercurio Peruano*, 4, 21 (1920), 161–73.
*Ensayos escogidos de filosofía y educación nacional.* Huancayo: Consejo
Provincial de Huancayo, Inspección de Cultura, 1967.
*Estética aplicada. Lo bello en el Arte: escultura, pintura, música (apuntes y
extractos).* Lima: Imprenta Americana, 1935.
*Estética aplicada. Lo bello en el Arte: la arquitectura (apuntes y extractos).*
Lima: Compañía de Impresiones y Publicidad, 1932.
*Estética aplicada. Lo bello en la Naturaleza (apuntes).* Lima: Rivas Berrio,
1929.
*Estética general.* Lima: Imprenta E. Rávago, 1923.
"Grados estéticos." *Mercurio Peruano*, 5, 28 (1920), 242–52.
"Ideas sobre la educación moral." *Mercurio Peruano*, 22, 159 (1940), 312.
"Informe presentado al supremo gobierno relativo a la reforma univer-
sitaria." *Revista Universitaria*, 1 (1930), 1–105.

"La actividad estética." *Mercurio Peruano*, 4, 24 (1920), 416–29.

"La belleza y el bien." *Mercurio Peruano*, 10, 58 (1923), 572–85.

"La cultura general y técnica." *Revista Universitaria*, 1 (1913), 301–12.

*La cultura nacional.* 2d ed. Lima: n.p., 1937.

*La cultura superior en Italia.* Lima: Librería Francesa Científica, 1912.

*La cultura superior en Suiza.* Lima: Imprenta A. J. Berrio, 1929.

"La escuela de cultura general." *Revista Universitaria*, 2 (1913), 232–46.

"La escuela de hoy y la escuela de mañana." *Mercurio Peruano*, 22, 158 (1940), 193–205.

*La estética de José Vasconcelos.* Lima: Taller Gráfico de Barrantese C., 1939.

"La estética de la libertad." *Mercurio Peruano*, 6, 32 (1921), 144–51; 7, 38 (1921), 17–28; 7, 44 (1922), 579–98.

"La experiencia estética." *Mercurio Peruano*, 4, 22 (1920), 267–79. Reprinted in *Revista de Filosofía* (Buenos Aires), 7, 2 (1921), 240–51.

"La instrucción primaria en la República Argentina." *El Peruano*, 2, nos. 13, 14, 29, 31, 37, 42, 66, 67, 68 (1898); 1, nos. 3, 6, 13, 14, 15, 16 (1899).

"La instrucción pública en Francia." *El Ateneo* (Lima), 3, 15 (1900), 283–303; 3, 16 (1900), 305–52; 3, 17 (1900), 405–38; 4, 21 (1901), 329–54; 4, 23 (1902), 429–58; 4, 24 (1902), 529–58; 4, 25 (1902), 629–69; 4, 26 (1902), 733–72; 5, 27 (1903), 833–72; 6, 28 (1903), 963–1005; 6, 29 (1903), 1063–82; 6, 30 (1903), 1167–96; 8, 39 (1907), 51–84; 8, 40 (1907), 172–88; 8, 41 (1907), 254–96.

"La reforma de la segunda enseñanza." *Revista Universitaria*, 1 (1916), 524–46; 2 (1916), 43–62.

*Las ideas de orden y de libertad en la historia del pensamiento humano.* 2 vols. Lima: Casa Editora Ernesto R. Villarán, 1919–22.

"Las leyes del trabajo mental." *Revista Universitaria*, 1 (1914), 315–25, 463–95, 548–49; 2 (1914), 1–35.

"Libertad y obediencia." *Revista Universitaria*, 1 (1913), 601–14.

"Lo bello en el arte." *Mercurio Peruano*, 6, 31 (1921), 6–25. Reprinted in *Revista de Filosofía* (Buenos Aires), 7, 4 (1921), 107–25.

"Lo bello en la naturaleza." *Mercurio Peruano*, 5, 30 (1920), 464–75.

*Los sistemas de moral; apuntes.* 2 vols. Callao: Empresa Editora de "El Callao," 1938–40.

"Moralidad y educación." *Revista Universitaria*, 2 (1913), 551–70.

"Reforma de exámenes de la Facultad de Letras." *Revista Universitaria*, 1 (1907), 48–52.

"Sobre la teoría del valor." *Revista de Filosofía* (Buenos Aires), 10, 2 (1924), 210–16.

"Un juicio crítico notable." *El Callao*, March 28, 1894. Reprinted in

*Colección de libros y documentos referentes a la historia del Perú, Tercera serie* (pp. 13–25). Lima: Librería e Imprenta Gil, 1941.

"Un libro notable." *Revista Universitaria*, 2 (1907), 337–416.

WORKS ON DEÚSTUA

Arízola Tirado, Gonzalo, et al. "Bibliografía de las obras del Dr. Alejandro O. Deústua." *Letras*, 13 (1939), 197–223.

Barboza, Enrique. "Las ideas pedagógicas de Alejandro O. Deústua." *Letras*, 13 (1939), 161–78.

Chiriboga, Julio. "Deústua y la filosofía de los valores." *Letras*, 13 (1939), 179–91.

Ibérico, Mariano. "Homenaje al Doctor Deústua." *Mercurio Peruano*, 11, 61–62 (1923), 51–62.

————. "La obra filosófica de Don Alejandro Deústua." *Letras*, 13 (1939), 145–60.

Miró Quesada, Francisco. "La filosofía del orden y de la libertad y su influencia práctica." *Letras*, 13 (1939), 192–96.

Romero, Francisco. "Breve noticia sobre Alejandro O. Deústua." *Luminar*, nos. 3–4 (1943), 310–16.


CRITICAL WORKS WITH COMMENTS ON DEÚSTUA

Ibérico Rodríguez, Mariano. "La universidad y la filosofía." *Mercurio Peruano*, 32, 290 (1951), 204–18.

Larroyo, Francisco. *La filosofía americana. Su razón y su sinrazón de ser* (pp. 120–23). México, D.F.: Universidad Nacional Autónoma de México, 1958.

Mariátegui, José Carlos. *7 ensayos de interpretación de la realidad peruana* (pp. 113–19). 2d ed. Lima: Biblioteca "Amauta," 1943.

Masur, Gerhard. "Corrientes filosóficas en América." *Revista de América*, 2 (1945), 130–35.

Miró Quesada, Francisco. "La filosofía en el Perú actual." *Cursos y Conferencias*, año 13, vol. 25, núm. 149 (1944), 272–84.

Peñaloza, Walter. "La filosofía en el Perú hasta Deústua." *Mercurio Peruano*, 22, 246 (1947), 411–24.

Salazar Bondy, Augusto. *La filosofía en el Perú. Panorama histórico* (pp. 35–40). Washington, D.C.: Pan American Union, n.d..

————. *Historia de las ideas en el Perú contemporáneo* (pp. 148–89). 2 vols. Lima: Francisco Moncloa Editores, 1965.

Sánchez Reulet, Aníbal, ed. *La filosofía latinoamericana contemporánea* (pp. 51–53). Washington, D.C.: Pan American Union, 1949.

RELATED WORKS

Basadre, Jorge. *Historia de la República del Perú*. 3d ed. Lima: Editorial Cultura Antártica, 1946.

Bergson, Henri. *An Introduction to Metaphysics*. Translated by T. E. Hulme. New York and London: G. P. Putman's Sons, 1912.

――――. *Creative Evolution*. Translated by Arthur Mitchell. New York: H. Holt & Co., 1911.

――――. *Matter and Memory*. Translated by Nancy M. Paul and W. Scott Palmer. London: S. Sonnenschein & Co.; New York: The Macmillan Co., 1911.

――――. *Time and Free Will*. Translated by F. L. Pogson. London: G. Allen & Co.; New York: The Macmillan Co., 1913.

Bocheński, I. M. *Contemporary European Philosophy*. Translated by D. Nicholl and K. Aschenbrenner. Berkeley and Los Angeles: University of California Press, 1964.

Borja, José Jiménez. "La universidad peruana en el siglo XX." In *Visión del Perú en el siglo XX*, edited by José Pareja y Paz-Soldán (vol. 2, pp. 127–38). Lima: Ediciones Librería Studium, 1962.

Bullough, Edward. " 'Psychical Distance' as a Factor in Art and an Aesthetic Principle." *British Journal of Psychology*, 5 (1912–13), 87–118.

Caso, Antonio. *La existencia como economía, como desinterés y como caridad*. 2d ed. México, D.F.: Secretaría de Educación Pública, 1943.

Chandrasekhar, Subramanyan. The Second Nora and Edward Ryerson Lecture, University of Chicago. Excerpts reprinted in *The University of Chicago Magazine*, 67, 4 (Summer, 1975), 4.

Comte, Auguste. *Positive Philosophy*. Translated by Harriet Martineau. 3 vols. 3d ed. London: G. Bell & Sons, 1896.

Crawford, William Rex. *A Century of Latin American Thought*. 2d ed. Cambridge: Harvard University Press, 1961.

Croce, Benedetto. *Aesthetics*. Translated by Douglas Ainslie. 4th ed. New York: The Noonday Press, 1956.

Davis, Harold Eugene. *Latin American Thought: A Historical Introduction*. Baton Rouge: Louisiana State University Press, 1972.

Dewey, John. *Art as Experience*. New York: Capricorn Books, 1958.

Ferreira, Carlos Vaz. *Lógica viva*. 2d ed. Buenos Aires: Editorial Losada, 1952.

González Prada, Manuel. *Páginas libres*. 3d ed. Lima: Ed. P. T. C. M., 1946.

Haddox, John H. *Antonio Caso. Philosopher of Mexico*. Austin & London: University of Texas Press, 1971.

Hegel, G. W. F. *The Philosophy of Fine Art*. Translated by F. P. B. Osmaton. 4 vols. London: G. Bell & Sons, 1920.

Kallen, Horace M. *Art and Freedom. A Historical and Biographical Interpretation of the Relations Between the Ideas of Beauty, Use, and Freedom in Western Civilization from the Greeks to the Present Day.* 2 vols. New York: Duell, Sloan & Pearce, 1942.

Korn, Alejandro. *Sistema filosófico.* Buenos Aires: Editorial Nova, 1959.

Krause, K. C. F. *Compendio de estética.* Translated by Francisco Giner. 2d ed. Madrid: Librería de V. Suárez, 1883.

Maslow, A. H. *The Farther Reaches of Human Nature.* New York: The Viking Press, 1972.

Pirandello, Luigi. *L'umorismo, saggio.* 2d ed. Firenze: Luigi Battistelli Editore, 1920.

Prado y Urgarteche, Javier. *Estado social del Perú durante la dominación española (estudio histórico-sociológico),* in *Colección de libros y documentos referentes a la historia del Perú, Tercera serie.* Lima: Librería e Imprenta Gil, 1941.

Rader, Melvin, ed. *A Modern Book of Aesthetics.* 2d ed. New York: Henry Holt & Co., 1952.

Reichenbach, Hans. *The Rise of Scientific Philosophy.* 11th ed. Berkeley and Los Angeles: University of California Press, 1964.

Ribot, T. A. *Essay on the Creative Imagination.* Translated by Albert H. N. Baron. Chicago: The Open Court Publishing Co., 1906.

Riva-Agüero, José de la. *Obras completas,* vol. 2. Lima: Pontificia Universidad Católica del Perú, 1962.

Stabb, Martin S. *In Quest of Identity: Patterns in the Spanish-American Essay of Ideas, 1890–1960.* Chapel Hill: University of North Carolina Press, 1967.

Thrall, William Flint, et al. *A Handbook to Literature.* New York: The Odyssey Press, 1960.

Torchia Estrada, Juan Carlos. *La filosofía en la Argentina.* Washington, D.C.: Pan American Union, 1961.

Villarán, Manuel Vicente. "Las profesiones liberales en el Perú." *Mercurio Peruano,* 39 (1958), 185–207.

Wimsatt, Jr., W. K. *The Verbal Icon.* New York: The Noonday Press, 1958.

Wundt, Wilhelm. *Outlines of Psychology.* Translated by Charles H. Judd. Leipzig: W. Engelman; New York: G. E. Stechert, 1897.

Zea, Leopoldo. *Dos estapas del pensamiento en Hispanoamérica; del romanticismo al positivismo.* México, D.F.: Colegio de México, 1949.

———. *El positivismo en México.* 2d ed. México, D.F.: Ediciones Studium, 1953.

# LATIN AMERICAN MONOGRAPHS—SECOND SERIES